ABOUT POSSESSION
The Self as Private Property

ABOUT POSSESSION

The Self as Private Property

John R. Wikse

The Pennsylvania State University Press
University Park and London

Library of Congress Cataloging in Publication Data

Wikse, John R
  About possession.

  Includes bibliography and index.
  1. Self.   2. Political science.   I. Title.
BF697.W493   155.2   77-1516
ISBN 0-271-00502-5

Designed by Gretl Yeager Magadini

Printed in the United States of America

Contents

How to Read This Book

This book is a meditation on the idea of the self as its own private possession. It is not an argument. It presents and attempts to make intelligible the perspective of the self as private property. Since I treat private property as a framework of assumptions about the nature of human interaction and value (what I call an "epistemological space") my concern is for the reader to see through this perspective. This book is a meditation on the language and logic of private property as basic structures of our collective lives. The patterns of assumptions through which we give order and meaning to our lives are our political theories, our ways of "seeing" the *polis*. The way of seeing the *polis* through the perspective of the private, separate person is a deep root of modern, Western political culture. To appreciate this perspective fully you must enter into it.

I use etymologies to evoke in the reader the associations which hold this perspective together. My etymologies are meditations from the perspective of the self as private property. For example, the verb "to appreciate" derives from the Latin *appretiare*, meaning "to set a price to." To meditate on this etymology is to gain access to the association between value and price which is central to the logic of private property. It is to enter that basically Hobbesian world in which the worth of a man is his price.

A meditation is an act of concentration and focus. It narrows and points to a center. My etymological meditations focus on the possessive and property-related roots of selected moral concepts in order to uncover associations of which we are, I think, commonly unconscious. This coherent set of associations about meaning and value which is organized around the logic of private property is what I call the "possessive unconscious." My intent is to get the reader "into" this perspective.

In this book I have traveled up many branches from the root which is about possession. It is but one root system. It is a perspective which I have lived. I ask you to enter into it and see yourself through it.

Acknowledgments

I began to study political theory at the University of California, Berkeley, during the time of rebellion in the middle to late sixties. During those years it became clear from my experience that to understand myself was a political activity. The illusion of the self separate from politics, and the idea that "politics" is "out there" and "I" am "in here," could not withstand the force of circumstances, the politicization of everyday life. The collapse of the distinctions between the political and the private, the society and the self, the citizen and the man, work and life altered the way I saw myself. The self which I had always thought I was—the private, separate ego, my "own" man—was clearly revealed as a social artifact, an ideology: the self as private property.

During my years in Berkeley I learned from many people. John Schaar thought I was incorrigible, but continued nonetheless to teach me that Kierkegaard wouldn't work: that in thinking about political things it was idiotic to begin with the self. Much that I have written here is a confrontation with this teaching. During the depth of my obsession with these ideas Hanna Pitkin directed my Ph.D. dissertation and taught me that not everything was about possession. Sheldon Wolin taught me respect for the vocation of political theory. Norman Jacobson taught me to think about politics in terms of sanity, and to respect my own experience. Many friends and political theorists contributed to my political education, among them Marge Frantz, Jeff Lustig, Doug Lummis, Michael Leiserson, Nancy Bardacke, and most important M. Brian Murphy.

André Orianne, Michael Weinstein, and Wilson Carey McWilliams each criticized and encouraged my work, forcing me to be clearer about what I meant to say. My colleague Larry D. Spence continues to teach me daily about what it means to be a political scientist, and how to survive the long march through our dying institutions.

Wanita Askey typed much of the manuscript. I received valuable editorial assistance from Willis L. Parker, despite his suspicion of etymological reconstructions of history. John M. Pickering supported and encouraged me in this work, reminding me that I had written a book when I was sometimes in doubt.

Linda Zanot refused to leave me alone during the writing of this book, despite my screams of laissez faire! She resisted and made me confront my idiocy by demanding that I see and respect difference. This is the gift of love and companionship.

JRW

Purdue Mountain, Pennsylvania

To My Mother and Father,

Bruna and Clarence Wikse

What ails me is the absolute frustration of my primeval societal instinct.... I think societal instinct much deeper than sex instinct—and societal repression much more devastating. There is no repression of the sexual individual comparable to the repression of the societal man in me, by the individual ego, my own and everybody else's.... Myself, I suffer badly from being so cut off.... At times one is forced to be essentially a hermit. I don't want to be. But anything else is either a personal tussle or a money tussle, sickening: except, of course, just for ordinary acquaintance, which remains acquaintance. One has no real human relations—that is so devastating.

—D. H. Lawrence

Introduction

The Production of Idiocy

This book is written out of the pain of my own idiocy, in the root sense of this word from the greek *idiotes*, meaning a private and separate person. Modern idiocy is a historically specific form of human identity, a mode of self-consciousness which emphasizes extreme individuation as the genuine foundation for being one-self. At the extremes of individuation, the essential characteristic of identity is that it is one's own. In my separation from others, in private and "alone with myself," deprived of others, this self with which I am alone is conceived on the logic of private property: it is my own unique possession, exclusively mine. I am concerned in these essays with the political theory and psychology of the self as private property.

This experience of identity is, I think, implicit whenever we think of the self as something which can be bought, sold, consolidated, stolen, bankrupt, given credit, or lost. The ideas of being "true to oneself," of being one's own person, of being a self-actualized individual each refer us to the assumption that what is essential about the self is its separation from others: that it is "ownness" or "mineness" which defines the experience of self. When it is extended into a philosophy of existence this idiocy is what we call "authenticity." To say that the logic of being authentic is the logic of private possession is to say that the idea of authenticity can be understood in its historical particularity as the subjective experience of the mode of production of modern capitalism.

My focus here is on the ideological structure, the pattern of coherence, the mode of identity of a way of productive and acquisitive activity which informs our most cherished conceptions of who we are, of our freedom and our sanity. Considered as an ideology, idiocy is a modern phenomenon. Though the idea of the *idion*, the private person, is present in classical antiquity (and other cultures), its organization into a structure of meaning, its dominance and pervasiveness as an assumption about the nature of being human, is modern in Western culture.

Our consciousness of the world is, as Nietzsche expressed it, "only a means of communication . . . evolved through social intercourse and with a view to the interests of social intercourse." Nietzsche understood social intercourse to include "influences of the 'outer world' and the reactions they compel on our side; also our effect upon the outer world" (*Power*, p. 284).* The organization of the interests of social intercourse is what I understand Marx to have meant when he described the dominant moral and political concepts of an epoch as images of the "very empirical fetters and restrictions within which the mode of production of life and [its] related form of interaction move" (*Young Marx*, p. 311). By this Marx meant that the way we work is reflected in the ideas we produce, in our conceptions, in our consciousness of ourselves as all these are manifested in the language of politics, law, morality, and metaphysics. In this reflection, independent philosophy loses its medium of existence and must always be connected to the concrete ways in which people interact to produce their living.

Thus there is no recourse from the banality of philosophy. There are only different ways of producing the facts of life. The philosophy of authenticity, its roots in the beginnings of industrial and entrepreneurial capitalism in the modern West, extends the logic of commodity production and fetishism to embrace even the self as one's own possession. This philosophy is deeply reactionary today: an overlay, an ideological remnant. It reacts and stands in sharp relief against the heavily corporate and bureaucratized work world and the cybernetic technology of the twentieth century. Viewed as an ideology, the idea of authenticity is rooted in the conception of "possessive individualism" which grew, as C. B. MacPherson has demonstrated, from Hobbes to Locke. In the history of modern Western political theory, Rousseau first articulates the problem and the ideology of authenticity, and it is with Rousseau that my discussion of the tradition of authenticity (Chapter 4) begins.

While John Locke could write in the eighteenth century of the man with property in himself, while Bentham could go in search of human nature (as Marx said) and discover the British shopkeeper, so today the most progressive moral and political philosophy and social theory agrees with Nietzsche and Marx that a man

---

*A list of Reference Titles and a Bibliography are at the end of this book.

2

is a relationship with others and the world, not a secret thing behind one's activities, in private. In terms of this perspective the idea of authenticity is an essentially conservative attempt to hold onto the freedom of private property in the face of the progressive "deprivatization" of consciousness which is implicit in seeing our*selves* as relationships, transactions, systems, processes or exchanges with others and the world. Lest we forget the banality of philosophy in our temptation to ontologize this process conception of identity, we might recall this recent advertisement for an expensive pair of shoes: "This isn't a shoe, it's a relationship."

To think about yourself as a process or a relationship is only an example of the truth that people think of themselves in terms of the productive metaphors of their times. All socioeconomic contexts result in particular modes of personal awareness or self-consciousness. Thinking about who you are is an activity of production, a social act. Thus the idea that the self is a kind of property, a substance which can be owned or exclusively possessed, is itself an idea produced in the mode of production of capital: that value or wealth which is capable of being accumulated and which, under a capitalist economy, is the active and productive principle of life. My concern in this book is with this mode of personal awareness.

This mode is giving way in the face of an increasingly cybernetic world, in which complex systems of information exchange and retrieval coordinate bureaucratically organized and geographically dispersed activities. The application of the principles of systems theory and cybernetic models to personal awareness involves the ability to think of the self not as a substance but as a process. Cybernetics aids in the study of relationships. Its formal concepts emerged during World War II in the context of Allied intelligence activities involving "systems that combined servomechanisms, computers, human beings, and the exigencies of war" (Parsegian, *Cybernetic World*, p. 4). Where human productive activity involves this level of complexity and cooperation, the Heraclitean flux is a more likely metaphor for identity than is private property because it is the system which is active and productive, which delivers the goods. (For a cosmology of process, see A. N. Whitehead, *Process and Reality*.)

What is coming to be known as "exchange theory" in the behavioral sciences reflects the transition between identity as property and identity as process. It is an attempt to get at the "fundamental processes of behavior" by calculating the "excess of the reward a person gets from an action over the costs he incurs," that is, "his profit or net reward from the action" (Homans, *Social Behavior*, p. 31). It turns out that the elementary forms of behavior happen to be the elementary forms of capitalist exchange. Homans argues (p. 1) that the profit metaphor conforms to "the intuitive notions men have concerning what determines their actions" and is indicative of the insights of common proverbs. His list of such insights reveals the focus of his research: "Every man has his price. Nothing succeeds like success. You can't eat your cake and have it too. Birds of a feather flock together. You scratch my back and I'll scratch yours. Do as you would be done by. To each his own. Fair exchange is no robbery.

No cross, no crown. *Noblesse oblige.* Whosoever hath, to him shall be given." Though Homans is aware of the "horrid profit-seeking implications" of his argument (which he does not discuss) and warns that it should not be dismissed out of hand on that account, it would appear that the argument is itself supportable *only* on those grounds. Homans's characteristic way of situating behavior is to say something like "Human affairs, especially economic affairs, are full of situations like this" (p. 53) and then describe an example, in this case that of two men who fear a rise in prices and start hoarding. Like Hobbes, Homans asks the reader to consult his own experience whereby elementary forms of social life are reduced to the subjective experience of a situation in which enduring social relations between people are limited by the psychology of possessive individualism. What Homans provides is thus an expression of the logic of private property as coterminous with the logic of human activity. The meaning of "exchange" in this sense is reduced to capitalist exchange. What Marx said about money should be applied to Homans's conception of this process: ". . . man as a social being must resort to exchange and . . . exchange—under the presupposition of private property—must end up in value. The mediating process of man making exchanges is no social, no *human process*, no human relationship; rather it is the abstract relationship of private property to private property . . ." (*Young Marx*, p. 267).

The struggle for sanity today has to do with whether you are yourself or another's. This choice is apparently so troubling to us that some of our contemporaries have concluded that we must discard personality (go mad) in order to escape it. Thus N. O. Brown (*Love's Body*, p. 161) embraces schizophrenic experience: "The solution to the problem of identity is, get lost." Brown understands how deeply the notions of person and private ownership are historically associated in the Western tradition:

> " 'Cain' means 'ownership.' Ownership was the
> originator of the earthly city." . . . Free persons . . . are
> those who own their own persons. It is because we own
> our persons that we are entitled to appropriate things
> that, through labor, become part of our personality or
> personalty. The defence of personal liberty is identical
> with the defence of property. There is a part of Karl
> Marx which attempts to base communism on Lockean
> premises. The Marxian proletariat is propertyless; they
> do not own themselves; they sell their labor
> (themselves) and are therefore not free, but wage slaves;
> they are not persons. The case against the notion of
> private property is based on the notion of person: but
> they are the same notion. Hobbes says a person is either
> his own or another's. This dilemma is escaped only by

4

those willing to discard personality. (*Love's Body*,
p. 146)

Brown sees that things are disintegrating, that the ideology of
the private, idiotic, separate self, the individual in isolation, is but
a convenient fiction. Instead (quoting the words of J. Riviere), the
self,

> ... that life of one's own, which is in fact so precious
> though so casually taken for granted, is a composite
> structure which has been and is being formed and built
> up since the day of our birth out of countless
> never-ending influences and exchanges between
> ourselves and others. .... These other persons are in fact
> therefore parts of ourselves. And we ourselves similarly
> have and have had effects and influences, intended or
> not, on all others who have an emotional relation to us,
> have loved or hated us. We are members one of another.
> (*Love's Body*, p. 147)

We live in a world in which, more and more, no one owns anything, and whatever private ownership still exists is separated
from political control. (See Berle and Means, *Corporation*.) Bu-
reaucrats produce procedures and rules, process people. Marx
wrote in his draft of *The German Ideology* that communism dif-
fered from all previous modes of production in that it involved the
conscious production of "the form of interaction" of society itself
(*Young Marx*, p. 462). The more we consciously produce not
commodities but modes of interaction or communication (though
these modes, like this book on the mode of possession, still retain
a commodity character and exchange value) the less we are able to
see ourselves as things to be held onto—but the more likely we
are to feel "lost" in the processes of institutions we do not control
(for instance, the mass-media depiction of reality, the procedures
of our bureaucracies). This process of "getting lost" is the most
advanced expression of the disintegration of modern society, the
most progressive development of *laissez faire*. To counsel that we
should get lost is to transform into an imperative the banal reality
of state capitalism. Along with the imperative "Be authentic!," it is
a redundancy to which we are already increasingly accustomed.
Have yourself or lose it, I would say, you will regret both.

Structured out of my own regret, this book expresses the painful
contradiction that the freedom to be one's own authentic self is as

5

well the idiocy and the poetry of private property. I have sought no way out, only perspective. This book should be seen as an attempt at a Marxist political psychology.

In the remainder of this introduction I want to illustrate in two different ways what I mean by becoming accustomed to idiocy: First, I will place this conception of identity into perspective with the classical Greek understanding of idiocy in order to gauge where we have come from. Second, I want to demonstrate how I learned to be an idiot.

Idiocy and Self-Sufficiency

Idiotic freedom, as I understand this concept from the perspective of the history of Western political theory, is the freedom of the solitary, private man. In the extreme it is the fantasy of the self-sufficiency of the individual, the project to complete and contain all meaning within the separate self. Aristotle taught that this image of man is deeply flawed, that the man who is isolated,

> who is unable to share in the benefits of political
> association, or has no need to share because he is
> already self-sufficient—is no part of the *polis*, and must
> be either a beast or a god. (*Politics*, Bk. 1, ii, #14, p. 6)

To think of the individual as self-sufficient was for Aristotle to pretend that an individual could be a *polis* unto himself. His self-sufficiency (*autarkeia*) was that condition which, by and of itself, "tends to make life desirable and lacking in nothing" (*Ethics*, Bk. 1, vii, #7, p. 24. Aristotle says that by "self-sufficiency" he means "not what is sufficient for oneself living the life of a solitary, but [it] includes parents, wife and children, friends and fellow-citizens in general.") Self-sufficiency is in this sense the fundamental category of politics, and the question of where a people locates the realm of self-sufficiency is the most fundamental political question. Individual self-sufficiency was the ground of political cynicism. The ideal of the Greek Cynics, as Barker has said, was the wise man "self-poised in his own *autarkeia* . . . the Cynic was sufficient to himself, and independent of everything outside himself" (*Political Thought*, p. 57). Such a thing was possible, Aristotle thought, only for a beast or a god, not for a human being who needed political association with others in order to be himself.

6

The Aristotelian critique of individual self-sufficiency (cynicism) is based on the assumption that only a life lived in political association with one's equals can be "desirable and lacking in nothing." To see oneself as the locus of self-sufficiency is, from this perspective, the arrogance of the part (the individual) pretending to be whole. Unless we acknowledge our need of others, our lives cannot be complete. This need is the ground from which human self-sufficiency is structured and upon which its possibility depends.

Aristotle's discussion of self-sufficiency is contained in his critique of Plato's *Republic*. Plato knew the temptation to cynicism from his own experience. He wrote about having withdrawn in disgust from the corruption of his times. In the *Republic* he speaks of founding a *polis* within the self, the city "in speech" (*logos*), built from the heavenly pattern of reasoned discourse, perhaps available to the man "who wants to see and found a city within himself on the basis of what he sees. It doesn't make any difference whether it is or will be somewhere. For he would mind the things of this city alone, and of no other." This foundation would locate the logic of politics (self-sufficiency) within the individual as that perfectly rational ideal which is one's own possession and which therefore no corruption or earthly misfortune could take away.

Aristotle understood correctly that the fundamental tendency of Plato's thought was toward unity (rather than toward plurality) and that the goal of unity was applicable more to an individual than to a city. For Aristotle, unity and self-sufficiency are opposite principles. To speak about politics with unity as the supreme value leads logically, Aristotle argues, to a focus on the individual, who can be "more of a unit" than a *polis* can be, since the city is an aggregation of different members contributing different things to one another (*Politics*, Bk. II, ii, #2, p. 41). Aristotle's critique of Plato is the basis for any critique of idiocy or cynicism: only *we* can be self-sufficient.

Plato's teaching was an attempt to transcend the *stasis*, the class conflict, contradictions and factions of the real Athens, which he knew to be a city divided against itself: a city of the poor and of the rich. The chaos, unpredictability, and blindness of the pursuit of wealth and the existence of the "poor man without means," which Plato called "the greatest of all evils" resulting from the rule of the wealthy few (oligarchy), is the pain of Plato's writing (*Republic*, #552a-b, pp. 229-230).

7

There is a sense of loss and desolation which pervades Plato's *Republic*. It is the loss of the *polis*, of the ancient city of Spartan simplicity. This city was preserved in thought by Plato to be consulted as the standard of ideal, rational political order through which the contradictions, futilities, and banalities of the everyday life of injustice could be transcended. Plato structured a political philosophy of consolation for the prudent and quiet man who bears up under personal sorrow, "taking this to be the part of a man . . . " (*Republic*, #605e, p. 289).

The greatest of Plato's sorrows was the spectacle procession of a "politics" in which ". . . beggars, men hungering for want of private goods, go to public affairs supposing that in them they must seize the good . . ." (*Republic*, #521a, p. 199). The fear that there is "no ally with whom one could go to the aid of justice and be preserved" (that everyone looks out for number one) leads to the temptation that a man could be content "if somehow he himself can live his life pure of injustice and unholy deeds, and take his leave from it graciously and cheerfully with fair hope" (*Republic*, #496e, p. 176). Being true to the ideal *polis* within you is the rational goal for cynics and puritans who hate the marketplace where everything is bought and sold. Plato, Rousseau, Emerson, and Nietzsche each explore the problems of having to select an identity in the marketplace way, whereby a man "would choose the sort that pleases him, like a man going into a general store of regimes" (*Republic*, #577d, pp. 235-236). Where all things can be bought and sold, have a price (including justice, character, and political office), and are amenable to cost-benefit accounting, there the nature of reason, the deliberative part of the soul, would be narrowed to a principle of calculation. Reason would come to be the consideration of nothing other than "where more money will come from less," as Plato put it. Where wealth is honored and admired, there pleasure will result only "from the possession of money and anything that contributes to getting it" (*Republic*, #553d, p. 231).

Plato recognized that the logic of the Athenian empire, torn between oligarchy and democracy, was defined so thoroughly by the logic of mine and thine that faction (*stasis*) was the rule within the city and the individual. The class strife which was the war of the city against itself was internalized within the individual, torn and divided against himself, driven by desires for "unnecessary and useless pleasures," watching the spectacle of "impeachments, judgements, and contests" of the battling oligarchs, who controlled the *polis* (*Republic*, #561a, p. 239; #565c, p. 244). In such a context, Plato believed, a good man would have to be a *polis* within himself. This *ek-static* vision of the transcendence of class conflict, this vision beyond *stasis* of the city within the self, is the classical political theory of idiocy and cynicism, the consolation of isolation in the face of desolation and loss.

It is my belief that increasingly this dilemma is our own: living in the decadent bicentennial of the American empire, torn between cynical disillusionment of the many and arrogant corruption of the wealthy few, people turn in upon themselves in the hope of transcendence and self-sufficiency. The value framework which results from this inward migration of the *polis* and this withdrawal of the logic of self-sufficiency within the individual is what we mean today by authenticity. It is what Aristotle would have called idiocy.

Plato knew that political socialization begins with the tales which are told to children in the nursery. Since I believe that we live in a world in which idiocy is a custom among us, I want to turn here to my own understanding of how I learned idiocy, to the earliest *music* (in the Greek sense of the word, which includes what we would call "stories") that I remember. Music in this sense is deeply political, as Plato knew, in teaching attitudes toward oedipal anger, authority, and emotional ambivalence (*Republic*, #387b-381e, pp. 56-59). Plato the poet and lawgiver laid down the political philosophy of idiocy as the rhythm which first attracted me to the study of politics. But I first learned that rhythm in a much more mundane way, and I was accustomed to it already when it spoke to me about what it meant to be a good man, about the importance of learning to live within myself. This idiocy is what I mean by self-possession.

I offer this autobiographical account of my idiocy on the assumption that its genesis is not idiosyncratically my own and in order to exemplify the Aristotelian understanding that we are political animals, that though we can think of ourselves as self-sufficient, self-reliant, self-actualized, and self-possessed, this very thinking refers us to a deep structure of political assumptions which we share with others despite what we might think of ourselves. In a culture of idiocy where the image of the private and separate individual is sold as an image of success and freedom, this deep structure is precisely what we share most deeply. Though the bonds which connect us to others, to place, or to principles may appear so unessential as to lead us to believe that our separation from others is our true existence, nonetheless we know that our most personal pains, problems, and ideals are public in the sense that they refer us to a shared political culture.

I was raised to be authentic, to be my own man. I was told that the way to success was to be self-possessed, to love difficulty and isolation, independence and self-sufficiency, as the strength of not needing others. I discovered the philosophy of authenticity as if I had lived it all along.

Cowboy Jack and the Learning of Self-Possession

My father, who taught me to be a man, often tells this story: He once had an abcessed tooth but refused the dentist's offer of novocaine; the dentist, digging around in my father's undrugged mouth, probing both the diseased root and his patient's apparent lack of pain, asked, "Doesn't that hurt?" My father replied, with total self-possession, "Of course it hurts."

Out of the depth of his own pain my father gave me a life-script, one which taught me that to be able to "take it" was to be a man: Control and possess pain within yourself, feel only beneath the surface, and hold onto your ability to control your own suffering as the basis of freedom and self-respect. Nobody can take away a man's ability to take it. Stoicism in the face of pain and punishment is resignation—of course it hurts to be a man.

I use the term "life-script" as it is used in transactional analysis to describe the logic and assumptions of life plans or patterns which are learned early in childhood through fables, myths, and stories which are lived out and performed as if they were pre-scripted by others. It was Plato's intent in the *Republic* to script the members of the guardian class against the possibility of experiencing anger against their fathers or among themselves, ambivalence about the gods, or desire to alter themselves in any way.

This life-script is a "successful" way of making a living in male culture. Emotional invulnerability, the discounting of pain, the capacity to take it are qualities which are highly praised in a man. "To be able to take it" must be understood in two senses: to be able to endure (survival) demands repression of the need to be open and vulnerable to others; it also demands holding oneself back, keeping one's life within oneself (self-possession). A successful man contains his needs, represses emotional dependence on others (particularly on other men), and displays a calm and collected exterior which demonstrates self-possession.

The more a man is able to take it, the more his life becomes his own, the more he becomes his own man. Being dependent on no one, he can be rejected by no one. Emerson first named the self-possessed individual the "self-helping man" and called him "living property," expressing the freedom of an identity which cannot be taken away because it is not dependent on others.

It was my life-script to become living property, to make myself into an object which I could hold onto and present to others as a complete, finished product, as my own independent and invulnerable self, lacking nothing. To become living property is to *behave* oneself in the most basic sense of that word, the root of which is the verb "to have." To behave oneself, I was taught, was to have oneself, to hold onto oneself, to hold oneself back from others. In performing my life-script, in behaving myself, I was making myself as much a piece of property as I could, making my living and my relations with others into living property and property relationships. Holding onto everything (myself, my wife, my job) out of the fear that I would lose myself, I tried to make my life into an inalienable object, to become a thing with an impermeable surface.

One of my male college friends, explaining that never to see me again would not affect him, once told me that he had come to see himself as a rock. The function of self-possession is to turn oneself into a thing, to live deep under the surface, never connected or profoundly related to others. Were I to leave or reject my friend, I could not touch him or hurt him—he could take it because he was a rock.

I was taught the ethos of self-possession through the earliest coherent story I remember, a bed-time tale which my father used to tell me, called "The Saga of Cowboy Jack." This story is both the most personal and intimate biographical fact of my life and my deepest connection to male culture. I relate it here in order to evidence the political psychology of self-possession, the assumptions about the nature of community and authority implicit in my learning to be a man. Here is my reconstruction of the story:

> Cowboy Jack is a stranger. He comes from nowhere,
> without a past, and ever wanders from town to town,
> riding his white horse, strong and self-reliant. In each
> town there is chaos, weakness, desperate need, and fear.
> An incompetent sheriff faces terrorizing bandits whom
> no one can identify. Everyone is at-a-loss. Though
> initially suspect and distant from the townspeople

because he is a stranger, this distance and strangeness also mean that Cowboy Jack has had no previous association with the town's evils. The people turn to him for advice and gradually Cowboy Jack discovers the root of the corruption and begins, unassisted, to save things. A heroic battle ensues in which the sheriff gets in the way and gets killed, but Cowboy Jack and the decent people emerge victorious. Amidst general joy Cowboy Jack is offered the job of sheriff and the sheriff's daughter (who has fallen irresistibly in love with him). Cowboy Jack lowers his head in deep gratitude, but with sadness for what he must renounce, declares that his journey is still unfinished, that there is still much work to do elsewhere, that he must ride on his way. Leaving the sheriff's daughter in tears, the townspeople wondering what they will do without him, and a friendly dog chasing after him, Cowboy Jack rides off into the sunset.

Each time my father told me this story I cried myself to sleep, sharing with him the understanding that of course it hurts to be a man, inferring many corollaries: Relationships with women, the experience of community, the possibilities of commitment and continuity in a place, genuine respect and gratification, all are separable from a man and his chosen work. Community is a stifling dependence on others, love is a fearful vulnerability (the sheriff's daughter), and if you stay and care and accept authority and connections with others, if you cease to be a stranger to others, then you're done for (the job of sheriff). Rather, do good deeds, live through your self-defined work, depend on no one, and you will be free.

From Emerson's self-helping man through Cowboy Jack, male culture in America has depicted the strength of self-possession as the key to a man's success. It has presented, as well, the price of that success: the renunciation of pleasure for a heroic struggle, the choice of work over love, of a stoical freedom over the possibilities of belonging. Self-possessed in a world of fearful dependence, you are a hero, a leader—others need you to save them. You will not be able to receive the love they offer, for you must remain a stranger to those you help—only as a stranger can you resist the evil, since the evil is dependence on others. Their love will go out to you because you appear not to need it; you are an authority and community unto yourself. You know only how to give (strength), not how to receive (weakness).

Thus in my yesteryears, I was taught that a real man is a masked man: the Lone Ranger. If others could see beneath the mask of self-possession, if they could come to know you in your real needs, they might reject you; a real man should not have needs. As a heroic stranger a man performs a mission of salvation; problems are *their* problems, needs are *theirs*, not one's own.

The logic of the Cowboy Jack life-script presupposes a world in which there are only persecutors, victims, and rescuers; and it teaches that only the rescuers are free. You cannot be victimized if you don't need others. A real man must be a rescuer, I was taught, his basic heroism being the renunciation of need and gratification.

The experience of being a performer best expresses the character of this renunciation. Most deeply associated with my work life, performance has meant for me a distancing and estrangement from others, based on the suppression, discounting, and denial of my needs. Performance is work done by a masked man who has separated his work from his needs for gratification. Performance is a way of making a living in which the fact that true work is always social, always done with and through other people, is denied.

This denial of the ways in which work entails dependence on others can, in the extreme, make the lived reality and presence of other people disappear. Holding myself back behind my work and relationships with others, performing my script, often has made others irrelevant to me. I once showed up early for a meeting of my men's group, at a time of great personal confusion. As I sat alone in the room in which we regularly met, I began to wonder whether the meeting had been moved or called off, whether I would be the only one there. Then, in genuine terror, I wondered whether everyone else was in fact there but that I couldn't see them. The realization struck me powerfully that, even in the most nurturing and supportive context I have known, I was frequently so self-possessed that others were not there for me and I was not there for them.

Men who work in institutions which are characterized by the rescue triangle [the "rescue triangle" has been studied by Steiner; see his *Scripts*], where rescuers, victims, and persecutors play out their various scripts (as teachers, students, and administrators, for example), necessarily experience the pain of performance. I was scripted to be a success in such an institution, taught that to succeed I must present a facade of invulnerability to other men, performing my work as a finished and perfect product, a performer immune to criticism and with no connection to the people with whom I work. In one of my first graduate seminars I was informed by the instructor that "ideas are property"; that my ideas are my own, not a product of the process of collective work and learning. In the academic work world, self-possession is part of the experience of work defined by the logic of commodity fetishism, which transforms the process of social work into a fixation on the finished, completed product. This product, offered for competitive evaluation by others, since it is an extension of oneself, must be invulnerable. To admit doubt and uncertainty or tentativeness about one of "my ideas" is to be, potentially, a victim; many teachers are fired for exactly this reason, that they questioned the worth and significance of their work. To begin to structure a context within which productive and gratifying work is possible is to cease to perform.

The separation of work as performance from work as gratification has profound consequences both for the quality of relationships between competitive male performers and for the nature of a performing man's expectations about women. Insofar as male culture has defined dominant work institutions as places where men work, the separation between work and women parallels the separation of performance from gratification. Since a man cannot have gratification in his work, he must turn to women as sources for it.

Simone de Beauvoir in *The Second Sex* noted the way in which the experience of being a woman is the experience of being "the other." From the pain and perceived necessity of being able to take it, I have often made women into objects of total gratification, their "otherness" being a projection of the needs, fears, doubts, and vulnerability I felt I had to renounce in order to be a man. But taking this attitude also means that to be drawn to a woman is to be drawn to what one fears in oneself.

In the sixteenth century, Thomas Hobbes wrote that men do not naturally take pleasure in one another's company. Though by "men" he meant humankind, this phrase—when applied to the experience of male work relationships of competitive performance—accurately describes the separation of work and gratification. The state of male performance relationships, like Hobbes's conception of the state of nature, is characterized by competition, enmity, and diffidence. To perform to the expectations of others is, in Hobbesian terms, to escape universal vulnerability by building a commodious life in which success and security rather than gratification ("the making of pleasantness") is the end and solo performances are the means; in which the self is a thing to be

THE PRODUCTION OF IDIOCY

possessed and others are things to be used.

There is a game which is played among men in this culture which exemplifies the logic of performance, the necessity of being able to take it, and the objectification of one man by another which is the prerequisite of the objectification of women. I call the game "the obscene greeting" game in memory of one of my college roommates who used such phrases in saluting his friends, often accompanied by a hard slap on the back or a quick punch in the belly. The game called for either stoical indifference to this greeting (I can take it) or retaliation in kind (I can give it back). This retaliative response cements reciprocal objectification in male interaction; it accepts the object-surface, the masked performance, as what can be shared among men. Hostility, aggression, mocking, and derision are forms of endearment among men and also ways of testing the strength of mechanisms of desensitization, tacitly sharing the understanding that being a man is based on being able to take punishment and give pain.

The dilemmas of growing up as Cowboy Jack are mundane. Yet, to be able to articulate the meaning of the most banal of my experiences is also to tap the systematic patterns, logics, and limits of my political culture. I will refer to these limits in the chapters which follow as the logic of behavior.

1
The Logic of Behavior

I hate myself for loving you
and the weakness that it shows . . .
I hate that foolish game we played
and the need that was expressed . . .
I've paid the price of solitude,
but at least I'm out of debt.
                    —Bob Dylan, "Dirge"

Told to behave herself, a two-year-old child replied
to her father: "I am being haved." (*Centre Daily*
Times, State College, Pa., April 3, 1976)

The constitution of human identity as a property relationship of
the self to the self is the logic of behavior. Where the logic of
private property is the integrating principle of the human personality, then the experience of individuation will be about property—possession. I have entitled this book *About Possession* because "possession" or "having" is the etymological root of our
word *behavior*, formed in the fifteenth century from the prefix *be-*
(about or concerning, intensively) and *haven* (to have or possess).
The Old English *behabban*, which meant "to restrain," provides
the original meaning of *behavior* as having oneself under one's
own control.

In arguing that possession is the logic of behavior I am attempting to radically distinguish *behavior* from our more generic term
activity. Behavior is, I think, historically a specific kind of activity.
My purpose is to clarify what "behave" means, to provide a con-
ceptual framework and a political perspective on what I will call
the "behavioral self," the self which understands itself as private
property.

The distinction between behavior and activity which I intend differs from that which Hannah Arendt draws in *The Human Condition*. For Arendt, "behavior" is basically an aggregate phenomenon involving great numbers, conformism, and automatism in human affairs. Behavior, she argues, removes the individuality from activity and makes possible the mathematical treatment of social reality (behaviorism). Behavior is from this perspective essentially a manifestation of mass society where individual, heroic deeds ". . . will have less and less chance to stem the tide of behavior" (*Human*, p. 40).

This distinction obscures what I think is the crucial characteristic of behavior as a kind of activity: the despair that unless I hold onto my authentic self, wrenching it away from the bog of social conformity, unless I possess myself truly, then I am at-a-loss. "Behavior" understood in this way refers to the framework of assumptions within which the separation of the heroic "self" from its "society" is possible.

My perspective on behavior is "archeological" in Michel Foucault's sense of the word. I have tried to uncover and describe the logic or pattern of coherence of what Foucault calls an epistemological space, a way of knowing specific to a particular culture and historical period. The epistemological space which is defined by the logic of behavior offers the perspective of what I have called "idiocy." The logic of this space, which includes idiocy and authenticity, is the logic of ownership and private possession. How does a private and separate person know the world, what does he think and see, how does he understand himself, his relationships, his freedom, his power? The answers to these questions articulate a pattern of coherence which, since the Renaissance and Reformation, gradually comes to constitute both the madness and the wisdom of modern Western political culture.

To say that our madness and our wisdom are of the same logic, that idiocy and authenticity share a common epistemological space, is to argue that the same rules or principles of ordering apply to experiences which are usually understood as mutually exclusive. We normally think that one cannot be both mad and wise simultaneously, sane and insane at one time. My concern here is to show that the psychopathology of the modern West and our philosophy of authenticity share the same basic logic of idiocy which provides a coherence of meaning to experiences which we usually distinguish as opposed.

Our foolishness, our folly, our seriousness, and our freedom involve the self-loving, affirming, developing individual. Michel

Foucault has commented on the symbolism of madness in the West since the fifteenth century:

> In this delusive attachment to himself, man generates his madness like a mirage. The symbol of madness will henceforth be that mirror which, without reflecting anything real, will secretly offer the man who observes himself in it the dream of his own presumption. (*Madness*, p. 27)

Idiocy is the dream of our own presumption, a mirage of the behavioral self, the meaning of our madness. Madmen first haunted the landscape of the modern West (and were depicted in our art and literature) in the fifteenth century, vagabonds carried into European market cities by merchants and sailors and "lost" or abandoned there. These wanderers, whose only location in the world was the "ship of fools" which transported them between cities, had no home, no craft, no pattern of dependable relationships to orient their actions. On the journey of madness the only fixed compass point is the self alone, and there is only oneself for a companion. To have oneself as one's best and closest friend and companion, to be oneself and no other, to observe oneself in the mirror of idiocy is the madness of modernity and the logic of behavior.

To think of behavior in this way is to treat it as a moral concept. By this I mean that the assumptions which are embedded in the activity of "behaving" can be understood as the resultant of our moral psychology. Here I mean *moral* in its etymological sense, from the Latin *mores*, meaning customs, habits, manners. Understanding behavior thus as a moral term unearths a doubleness about "behavioral" psychology: that the reason and the madness of behavior are of the same logic.

That there is a logic to our moral (customary) psyche which is also the logic (the etymology) of the concepts which carry our moral inheritance is a basic assumption of this book, an intuition from Nietzsche's question,

> What light does linguistics, and especially the study of etymology, throw on the history of the evolution of moral concepts? (*Morals*, p. 55)

The etymology of moral concepts carries the collective history of a culture, the record of its assumptions preserved and developed in its changing significations. But this history is unconscious and repressed. To make it conscious and to act it out is to uncover the basic assumptions upon which a culture is constituted. To act out the logic of the moral unconscious is to be judged pathological by those members of a culture (most of us) who are accustomed to seeing these presumptions as truth. To extend the logic of the moral unconscious of a culture into a systematic, reasoned philosophical system is to do what we in the West have called, since Plato, political philosophy: to make our assumptions reveal their truths, to transform them into myths, to call them (as Plato did) noble lies. That the psychopathology and the political philosophy of a culture and the etymology of its moral concepts are of the same logic is the basic claim of this chapter. That the logic of behavior is about possession is a conclusion drawn from this integrated perspective.

The Prehistory of Behavior

Nietzsche used etymology as a method of gaining access to what he called the prehistory of a people, the morality of *mores* which for him was the basic principle of civilization: that any custom is better than no custom at all. This prehistory was not deeply hidden; rather he thought that it was present in all ages, or always likely to emerge in the moral ideals of a culture. It was for him "the workshop where ideals are manufactured." Moral ideals, Nietzsche thought, were always the ideals of the masters, superimposed on the powerless. Thus the origins of the moral concepts of all cultures divided by the logic of master and slave were with those who ruled:

> The lordly right of giving names extends so far that one should allow oneself to conceive the origin of language itself as an expression of power on the part of the rulers. (*Morals*, p. 26)

Thus domination was implicit in the history of moral terms and the peculiar privilege of a moral animal, to inherit a set of customs, contained a special danger:

> Not only the reason of millennia, but their madness too, breaks out in us. It is dangerous to be an heir. (*Zarathustra*, p. 189)

19

Only the human (the moral) animal can be in danger; and the essence of danger, as its etymology suggests, is domination. Our word *danger* shares a root with the Latin *dominiarium*, a derivative of *dominium*, meaning lordship or mastery, whence our word *domination*. In its archaic usage from the thirteenth century, danger (Old French *dangier*) meant the condition of being dependent upon a lord or master. The word *dan* was a term of honorific address or title given to a lord, and it is from this root that *danger* was formed. Being dependent on a dan, being in his power or indebted to him, was expressed as being "in danger." Only a moral animal can be indebted to a master, or to an ancestor—can come, as we say today, to owe a debt to society. It was, for Nietzsche, the "consciousness of indebtedness" to the domination of our ancestors which is the danger of inheritance.

The relationship between indebtedness and custom is also evident from an etymological perspective: our word *custom* derives from the Anglo-Norman *custume*, a service due from feudal tenants to their lord (or dan), a debt in kind or money, a tax or tribute. Thus debt is at the root of custom; being indebted is our customary danger. The history of Western culture can be seen as the gradual process of becoming moral in the sense of learning to repay debts, learning to be credible. The moral animal is believable. But the language of credibility is also the language of credit, both words deriving from the Latin *creditum*, a loan or thing entrusted to another. The workshop where our ideals are manufactured is, in other words, a customs house, and we are customers all.

This archaic heritage, our moral roots in the logic of credit and debt, suggests that, as Nietzsche put it, "the most primitive personal relationship" and therefore the basic relationship between a community and its members is that of indebtedness (*Morals*, pp. 70-71). Here, etymology reveals that the custom character of morality is about indebtedness, that the psychology of debt is the archaic legacy of our prehistory, always present in our moral or social psychology. It is also our danger, the haunting history of human domination whereby we learned how to repay. It is the root of the desperation of the debtor which modern Western psychology seeks to overcome.

Historically, the vulnerability of the debtor, his danger, is preserved in the records of customary punishments for failure to repay one's debt, whereby substitute payment to a lord consisted of whatever else the debtor might control, "his body, his wife, his freedom, or even his life" (*Morals*, p. 64). Failure to repay a community elicited the punishment of exile, of subjection to the wretchedness of one who had sundered his relationship to the social whole. Being separated from community was, Nietzsche thought, the root of wretchedness. He noted that the German *Elend* (wretchedness) originally meant exile; in parallel, the root of the English word *wretch* is the Old High German *reccheo*, exile.

The relationship between the language of morality and profit in Homeric Greece has been studied closely by Bruno Snell (*Discovery*, Ch. 8, "A Call to Virtue"). Snell concludes that the words "for virtue and good, *arete* and *agathos*, are at first by no means clearly distinguished from the area of profit" (p. 158). Snell writes: "Whether we are dealing with 'an eye for an eye' or with the custom of blood feud, the 'just' penalty is reckoned in figures, and ... the [damages] must be commensurate with the amount of damage perpetrated by [the delinquent]. As profit was amenable to prediction and calculation, so also the measures and degrees of justice" (p. 161).

The process which Nietzsche delineates is that by which economic exchange and barter, the contriving of equivalences, the measuring of person against person, the ethic of repayment, came to be a preoccupation so great that "everything has its price; all things can be paid for." The development of relationships of indebtedness, which characterized interpersonal relations in archaic community and which reinforced the advantages of communality, has been studied extensively by anthropologists beginning with Marcel Mauss and more recently continued with the work of Karl Polanyi and his students. What Polanyi referred to as the archaic economy of reciprocity is defined by the obligation to give in repayment to others. Polanyi demonstrated that during most of human history the realm of economics was "embedded" in social relations, but that with the birth of the self-regulating market, this relationship becomes inverted: "Instead of economy being embedded in social relations, social relations are embedded in the economic system" (*Transformation*, p. 57).

Marcel Mauss, in his *Essai sur le don*, documented the ways in which the obligation to give in order to humiliate others functions in ancient cultures as what he calls a "total" phenomenon, one that is economic, aesthetic, mythological, and social. This totality is termed by Mauss the "gift economy," and what makes the gift a totalizing metaphor is its connection with human identity; in rituals of exchange,

It is the veritable *persona* which is at stake, and it can
be lost in the potlatch just as it can be lost in the game
of gift-giving. . . . (*Gift*, p. 38)

To give, Mauss argues,

. . . is to show one's superiority, to show that one is
something more and higher, that one is *magister*. To
accept without returning or repaying more is to face
subordination, to become a client and subservient, to
become *minister*. (*Gift*, p. 72)

Mauss traces the logic of indebtedness through its various expressions in ancient culture. He suggests that the meaning of the
gift as it characterizes the "distinctive sphere of our social life" is
expressed in the "dangerous" etymology of the word: *gift* (French
le don, Greek *dosis*), a dose of poison. The English etymology of
our word *gift* reflects precisely the same sense: from Old English
gift, payment for a wife; from Old High German *gift* (feminine)
wife, (neuter) poison.

The gift economy which this etymology expresses is one in
which, as Mauss puts it, "sub-groups . . . are constantly embroiled
with and feel themselves indebted to each other" (*Gift*, p. 31).

The institutions of the gift economy, compared across cultures,
reveal what Mauss calls the "same kind of social and psychological pattern."

Food, women, children, possessions, charms, land,
labour, services, religious office, rank—everything is
stuff to be given away and repaid. (*Gift*, p. 31)

The theme that it is dangerous to receive a gift (which Mauss
traces from ancient Annamite culture through Emerson's essay
"On Gifts and Presents"), that one must always return more than
one receives, that charity wounds the receiver, leads Mauss to
conclude:

Our whole moral effort is directed toward suppressing
the unconscious harmful patronage of the rich almoner.

What Mauss calls the "basic imperialism of men" is expressed
in the fact that

> ... in the distinctive sphere of our social life we can
> never remain at rest. We must always return more than
> we receive. (*Gift*, p. 63)

With respect to interpersonal relationships, it is Mauss's thesis that the meaning of the gift economy, the perpetual cycle of indebtedness, perpetuates relations of dominance and submissiveness (of danger) and that social responsibility is that process by which people calculate their position along this dimension of indebtedness.

This pattern, Mauss hypothesized, has become secularized and rationalized in modernity, and this development meant for him that man had gradually become a "calculating machine"—*homo economicus*. Economic man is then, for Mauss, the culmination of the history of the gift economy, though the legacy that the gift is poison, expressed in ancient culture in terms of group identity, is recapitulated in modernity through the metaphor of "individual interest."

The thrust of Mauss's work is the unearthing of our moral psychology: that indebtedness is the substance of relationships of dominance and submissiveness, that freedom "in the gift" has historically been reinforced by "enslavement for debt" as the sanction for failure to repay (*Gift*, p. 41). Mauss's research established, in other words, the historical, etymological, and psychological priority of indebtedness as the basis of archaic moral considerations.

It was Nietzsche who first understood that the logic of archaic economics, of giving and indebtedness, comes in the modern West to be internalized within the self. The principle of giving and particularly the ability to reciprocate in the repayment of gifts was for Nietzsche the basis of communal solidarity in prehistory. He wrote, in a fragment on the "dual prehistory of good and evil," that among the ruling tribes and castes of primitive cultures a person is good by belonging to the "good," to a "community that possesses communal feeling because all individuals are knit together by the sense of repayment." As a moral principle, the ability to give preserves community.

Out of the danger, restraint, and punishments of the morality of customary indebtedness came the promise, Nietzsche thought, of autonomy, of

> ... the sovereign individual, like only to himself,
> liberated again from the morality of custom, autonomous

and supramoral (for "autonomous" and "moral" are mutually exclusive). (*Morals*, p. 59)

This autonomy was what Nietzsche announced as "the internalization of man," which he describes in terms of the project of wanting to become a gift or sacrifice, wanting to "pile up all the riches in your soul," to take all things into the individual. To locate giving within the self, to *become* a gift, is to take the principle of archaic community within the self.

An etymological view of the meaning of *community* reinforces this analysis. The most accepted derivation of our word *community* is from the Latin *munis*, gift, and *com-munis*, common, which appears to have been cognate with the Old Teutonic word *ga-main-z*, the root of the modern German word *Gemeinschaft* (community) which, since Weber, we have used in contrast to *Gesellschaft* (modern society). This distinction suggests that the interior of the individual comes to take on, in the modern West, the functions and characteristics of community, that the modern Western self-regulating market economy, sundered from *Gemeinschaft* relationships, relocates these relationships within the self-regulating individual. The burden of internalizing community within oneself, or taking the logic of social indebtedness within where it cannot be repaid, is for Nietzsche the burden of guilt. Here he employed etymology to underscore this perception, emphasizing that the German word for guilt (*Schuld*) had its origin in the "very material concept" of debts (*Schulden*) (*Morals*, pp. 62-63). [That guilt is the internalization of debt is central to my interpretation of Kierkegaard and Heidegger; see Chapter 4 in this book.] The English etymology of guilt appears to follow the same sense development as does the German. Old English *gylt* is used to render Latin *debitum* in the Lord's Prayer. From this it has been inferred that the primary sense of Modern English *guilt* may be debt.

The modern burden of guilt is, from this perspective, the internalization of the archaic legacy of indebtedness as a relationship with oneself. Nietzsche asked the question "How is guilt possible?" and answered that it was possible only as an experience "derived from nature or society and projected into the sphere of the 'in-itself' " (*Power* p. 311). I will discuss Nietzsche's understanding of this conclusion in detail below. Here it is enough to say that the man who is "like only to himself," who has the criteria of measure and evaluation within him, self-contained standards by which he posits his values, is beyond all need and dependence, all indebtedness to others: he is the man who is his own possession. Guilt, the price which we pay for the internalization of man, is the price of solitude; but at least we are out of debt.

These examples express well the function which etymology performs: it deontologizes moral philosophy by revealing the ways in which our moral concepts are grounded in experience and activity, despite their false projection into the essence of things. In other words, etymology reveals the psychology of guilt as a moral psychology.

From this perspective, the wisdom of a culture is an expression of that culture's particular moral obsessions, the fragments through which it justifies and gives meaning to its activities. In deontologizing moral value, Nietzsche does not simply refuse to believe in a realm of some essential "Being behind the doing" (*Morals*, p. 45) but rather explores the psychological utility of such a realm:

> All the values by means of which we have tried so far to render the world estimable for ourselves and which then proved inapplicable and therefore devaluated the world—all these values are, psychologically considered, the results of certain perspectives of utility, designed to maintain and increase human constructs of domination—and they have been falsely *projected* into the essence of things. (*Power*, p. 14)

In this way the question of the morality of an action is to be understood not in terms of the cause or motive behind it (not of a person's intent) but rather as a residue of human custom. Nietzsche's genealogical perspective on morals considers the question "How should one act?" as a result rather than a cause of human activity: "Morality follows; the ideal comes at the end" (*Power*, p. 228). The morality of intentions—the idea that an individual is morally accountable for his actions, that autonomy and responsibility, subjectivity and conscience, are attributes of people who choose and decide how they ought to act—is, Nietzsche thought, a particularly modern result of human activity. The ideal of individual moral autonomy presupposed the fact that danger and domination had become internalized, that the morality of the modern West would not be rooted in indebtedness to others, but in becoming indebted to oneself alone. That we carry domination around with ourselves, that we do it to ourselves, that we behave ourselves is the fact of our authenticity.

The Etymology of Behavior

Authenticity is a cultural fact. The experience of "inauthenticity," of being not autonomous, not responsible, not one's own person, is intelligible only on the assumption that the self is something of its own, which can be lost or alienated. The assumptions that one can possess oneself, master and control oneself, have a relationship with oneself, be not oneself are "behavioral" assumptions; that is, they are about possession. The ideal of authenticity is thus a result of a specific moral context, a conclusion of a way of living, a reference to what we are doing rather than what we "ought" to do. The fact of authenticity, like all moral facts, is a description of the pain of a particular mode of domination, a description of a way of life which is the wisdom and the madness of a given cultural context, projected into an ontological claim—in this case that the self is essentially something capable of being its own.

Etymology here again deontologizes the facts, teaching that wisdom is custom. A wise man sees the ways of his culture; our adjective *wise* is akin to the Old English noun *wise*, which meant the "ways," manners, customs, and habits of a place. These ways are the facts of political culture, its products or artifacts, its moral heritage. The etymological root of our word *fact* is the Latin *factum*, past participle of *facere*, to do or to make. Facts are fashioned (etymologically: from the same root, *fashion* meaning "what is customarily done"); facts are made up by factions or political cults (*fashion* and *faction* are synonymous at the root). What is fashioned is fashionable: if "it's just not done!," then it's not a fact. A political culture worships its own facts: a culture is a cult (etymologically: both from Latin *colere*, to honor with worship).

The concepts through which we express what is done, what is proper or appropriate, are revealing of the fundamental facts of our culture, and these moral concepts carry, from their etymological roots, the logic of our political cult, the reason and the madness which we have worshiped, the ways which are about possession.

Thus to pose the question "What is the meaning of the phrase *appropriate behavior*?" is to probe the history of the association of a cluster of terms which express the facts of our culture. These words crystallize our ways or customary activities. To understand

84306

that way or activity which we symbolize as "behavior" is to refer to the semantic history, the genealogy of the concept.

Today we use the words *improper* and *appropriate* to distinguish different behaviors. Yet, as William Galt has noted, "in studying etymological derivations we find many words standing alike for both terms of [a] moralistic dichotomy." Galt suggested that etymological analysis of moral dichotomies revealed a "preconscious sense in man of the basic identity between any two terms of a symbolic, moralistic dichotomy" ("Our Mother Tongue"). So it is with the etymological perspective on the apparent dichotomy between the improper and the appropriate: both words derive from the Old French verb *aproprier*, the verb *to improper* coming from the Middle English *empropre*, synonymous with the verb *to apropre* meaning to assign as a private possession, to appropriate. In the sixteenth century, an "impropriation" (or "appropriation") referred to the annexing of an ecclesiastical property by a lay individual. At the root of the adjectival forms is the activity of individual appropriation, the lay possession of church tithes, which characterized the Protestant Reformation. Appropriation is the basic identity beneath the moralistic dichotomies of our world of "propriety," uniting the proper (or appropriate) and the improper in the logic of possession.

The logic of property and the logic of propriety are the same: etymologically both words are from the French (late fifteenth, early sixteenth centuries) *propriété*, meaning the fact of being one's own, "ownness," the right of possession. The organization of the logic of possession into a coherent conception of human activity is reflected in the etymology of the four modern Western expressions of how people act: their demeanor, deportment (or comportment), conduct, and behavior.

Demeanor derives from *demesne*, belonging to a lord, a differentiated spelling of *domain*, belonging to a lord (*dominus*). Etymologically, *demeanor* is to *demesne* as *dominance* is to *domain*: how one does relates to what one has. Our word *deportment* (and *comportment*, less frequent in English but cognate with the modern French equivalent of *behavior*) derives from Latin *portare*, to carry, in the sense of "carrying oneself" or "bearing oneself" (one's "carriage"): ourselves are the property we carry around with us. Our word *conduct* derives from *conducere*, to collect or bring together, in the sense of "Collect yourself!," "Get it together, man!," that is, with the sense of self-control or mastery as in "cool and collected." What is collected in conduct, what is borne in deportment, the sort of demeanor one *has*, as the etymology of our word *behavior* suggests, refers us to the possessive root of our cultural norms.

Our word *behave* was formed in the late fifteenth century from the word *be-* (an intensive, originally meaning "about," more figuratively in the sense of "thorough"), and *have* (verb) in order to express a qualified sense of having, particularly in the reflexive: "to have or bear oneself." Our word *behavio(u)r* derives by form analogy with *havour*, common fifteenth- and sixteenth-century form of the Old French *aveir*, *avoir*, in the sense of having or possession. The logic of human reflexivity, the way we relate to ourselves, is, for the modern West, about possession.

These etymologies point us toward the morality of everyday life, toward the customary roots of our dichotomy of good and evil, toward the meaning of our ways, toward the limits or measures of what we consider appropriate. Good and evil are customary limits, as their etymologies indicate. Our word *evil* derives from the Middle English *uvel*, the Old German *übel*, both referring to the root meaning of "up or over" in the sense of exceeding due measure or proper limits; the root of our word *good* is from the Old Teutonic *god*, meaning fitting, suitable, appropriate. *God is good:* what we worship is what is appropriate. The proper limits of the good are the limits of appropriate behavior, and these limits are, for the modern West, about possession. Language carries our moral or social unconscious; etymology uncovers it—a tool, as Nietzsche knew, for a genealogist of morals.

In this perspective on the relationship between etymology and morality there is the assumption that the logic of a culture is a one-sided accentuation of a way of acting in and knowing the world. The etymologies of the symbolic dichotomies of our moral concepts reflect the one-sidedness which Marx described as the stupidity of extending the logic of private property to all human relations, wherein the possibilities of our consciousness of ourselves and the world—our "seeing, hearing, tasting, feeling, thinking, perceiving, acting, loving" as Marx said, come to have meaning "only as *immediate*, exclusive *satisfaction* or as *possession*, as having" (*Young Marx*, p. 307). For Marx, this one-sidedness was at the root of modern alienation. Thus he wrote:

> . . . *all* the physical and spiritual senses have been
> replaced by the simple alienation of them *all*, the sense
> of *having*. (*Young Marx*, p. 307)

The one-sidedness of possession makes us into what Nietzsche called "inverse cripples," as we project an inadequate and partial perspective into the essence of wisdom. But the condition of being inverse cripples is what we understand as normal or good or right. It is the basic contention of this book that the norms of modern Western political culture are so thoroughly connected to the logic of possession as to be unconsciously determined by it. The etymological parallels between the English *good* and *goods*, the German *gut* and *Güter*, the French *bien* and *biens*, suggests something of the depth of the relationship in Western culture between what is good and what can be possessed.

This perspective, which brings Nietzsche and Marx together, was expressed by the American psychologist Trigant Burrow, who maintained that the unconscious is social and that our forms of social adaptation are neurotic. The social neurosis of Western culture was, Burrow wrote, "the unconscious element underlying the psychology of the normal" characterized by "the pride in possession" (*Social Basis*, p. 15). That the neurotic and the normal are characterized by the same psychology, that of the social (or moral) unconsciousness of a culture, is fundamental to my perspective in this book.

What I mean here is that culture is defined by the limits and meanings of its customs, of its past carried with them, and is embedded especially in its linguistic institutions which are the deepest representations of its social or moral unconscious. The linguistic representations of social/moral psychology define the epistemological space within which our cultural experience has meaning. To say that cultural limits can be neurotic is only to emphasize the partiality, the one-sidedness, which is at the root of our freedom and our slavery.

The Psychopathology of Behavior

Maurice Merleau-Ponty, arguing (*Acquisition*, pp. 64, 68-69) that the normal and pathological "can be considerably enriched by the contact of one with the other," suggested that it was legitimate to interpret the normal in the light of the pathological since

> [if] . . . confusion exists in the pathological state, it is because it already exists in an embryonic form in the normal person. In the normal person, there is already a germ of alienation. . . .

29

Cross-cultural research in clinical psychology increasingly cor-roborates this understanding that there is a continuity between culturally sanctified modes of adaptation and the psychopatholog-ical disturbances characteristic of cultures. Draguns and Phillips, for example, suggest that there is plausibility to the view that "dis-turbed individuals act out the dynamic preoccupations of their culture," that "the thoughts, wishes and fears of normal members of a society are behaviorally expressed by the disturbed individu-als in their midst" ("Culture and Psychopathology").

Research on the language of schizophrenics in Western culture suggests that certain expressions which are symbolic or abstract for normal speakers of the language are actual and concrete for the schizophrenic. Thus William White observed that with respect to the experience which we refer to when we say that we "collect our thoughts" (an expression of the etymological sense of *conduct*), the schizophrenic individual attempts to actually gather his thoughts with his hands: he acts out the symbolic abstraction. Where we say that someone "puts his whole soul into his work," a schizophrenic experiences this abstraction, White notes, as "a concrete loss of a part of himself" ("The Language of Schizo-phrenia").

Since Alfred Storch, Western clinical psychology has em-phasized that the schizophrenic individual develops a language characterized by feeling states, concreteness, and perception rather than "reasoning, differentiation and abstraction" ("The Primitive Archaic Forms . . ."). What is expressed abstractly and symbolically by adapted members of a culture appears to be acted out concretely in its psychopathology.

But the inability to participate in the symbolic abstractions of one's own language does not necessarily involve the inability to abstract. In *Le Schizo et les langues*, Louis Wolfson, an American schizophrenic, writes of his obsession to annihilate his mother tongue. His problem is that he can no longer bear the pain of hear-ing and speaking English. He writes predominantly in French, but builds a vocabulary from the phonetic associations of French, German, Russian, and Hebrew words. He cannot adopt another tongue, but writes in many tongues (or no tongue at all) at once, in what has been described as a "one-man language" (Ausker, "One-Man Language").

A one-man language, like a one-man culture, is an impossibility. To attempt to possess or create within oneself an idiosyncratic or private language contradicts the communicative essence of language. Yet this psychopathology is but an extreme expression of the basic assumption about sanity in modern Western culture: that to be healthy and sane an individual must be self-possessed, must have or possess himself (behave). In this sense psychopathology can be seen to mirror the psychology of the normal at its extreme.

Alexander Lowen, a Reichean psychologist, has presented a description and analysis of schizophrenia which illuminates this relationship between the pathological and the normal in modern Western culture. Lowen writes:

> The schizophrenic acts as if he were "possessed" by some strange force over which he has no control. Before the advent of modern psychiatry it was customary to regard the insane as being "possessed by a demon" or "devil"—for which he was to be punished. We have rejected this explanation of his illness, but we cannot avoid the impression that the schizophrenic is "possessed." . . .

Thus for Lowen, to be possessed, to be taken over, to be out of oneself is the basic aspect of schizophrenia. Lowen recognizes how important the concept of "possession" is with respect to our understanding of the psyche:

> It is significant that we use the concept of "possession" in our language to designate sanity. We describe a person as being "in possession of himself" or "in possession of his faculties," or oppositely we say that he has "lost possession of himself."

Lowen notes that to be sane is to possess oneself, to be one's own person, to be self-possessed, and he defines self-possession in this way:

> Self-possession can be gauged by the person's ability to respond appropriately to his life situations. The schizophrenic lacks this ability completely. (*Betrayal*, p. 55)

For Lowen, self-possession is appropriate behavior, sanity and madness are about possession. But self-possession is "appropriate" only in response to quite specific life "situations," wherein possession is the logic of what is fitting or appropriate.

31

Mary Barnes, a schizophrenic woman, gives this description of the despair which is about possession:

> To be loved was to be possessed. To give myself up.
> Then came the absolute despair . . . the condition
> imposed upon me with regard to the giving and
> receiving of love was the loss of self. [Love meant] I am
> coming in on you, I shall possess, steal you, you will be
> no more. . . . The hospital with its drugs and compulsory
> admission is controlling and possessing. . . . I was
> starving for myself. (*Mary Barnes*, pp. 154-157)

That the self can be possessed, lost, given up, stolen are possibilities only for the "behavioral" self, which relates to itself as property. A young schizophrenic woman puts the basic assumption of the logic of behavior this way:

> If I weren't self-possessed I'd be nowhere, because I'd
> be mixed up in a medley of other things. (*Sanity*, p. 44)

Gregory Bateson once posed this question for the cultural sciences: "How are babies prevented from becoming exaggerated versions—caricatures—of the cultural norm?" The perspective of this book explores the opposite question: What do the exaggerations, the caricatures of the normal, tell us about the logic of a political culture? The exaggeration of the logic of possession is what I will call "behavioral despair." This despair is not an aberration: it is, I think, the logical extension of the confusion of the self and property, of identity and possession.

Behavioral Despair

I do not intend "property" here to denote material things, nor do I mean that the "confusion" between the self and property has to do with an identification between ourselves and the objects through which we extend ourselves into the world, where a threat to the object is a threat to the self. I am not speaking about the experience of being indistinguishable from what one possesses. Behavioral despair runs deeper than the concern for the loss of a valued object. Rather, it is the experience of one's relationships with others and with oneself, of the very process of identity, as essentially possessive. It is the experiences of power, freedom, friendship, and community as about possession.

Behavioral despair is the experience of relationships as necessarily involving a possessive calculation of the balance between credit and debt, as the striving, where it is most fully developed in the political philosophy and psychopathy of the modern West, for total self-possession. Here is an expression of the extreme logic of behavioral despair, a statement by one of Freud's students about the best way to live:

> I love only free people, those that are independent of
> me. For those who depend upon me make me
> dependent—for this I revenge myself, and then become
> guilty toward those who did me good. The guilt,
> however, eats up the capital, because it bears negative
> interest of immeasurable dimensions if one wants to pay
> one's debts. One cannot be bankrupt too often—I have
> already lost much of my credit. . . . The way I am living
> now is truly the best . . . : independent because nobody
> depends on me, not a slave because not a master.
> (*Brother Animal*, p. 17, quoting Victor Tausk)

The self which holds its independence as capital to be stored up against the possibility of bankruptcy, which experiences dependence upon others as the loss of that which is one's own, can never repay its debts and invariably loses its credit with others. The acquisition of inevitable guilt is the logical despair of the behavioral self. Where people cannot acknowledge their fundamental indebtedness to others without the threat of bankruptcy, possession, or loss, without the fear of giving in to others or throwing away (wasting) oneself on them, then this unacknowledged indebtedness is taken into the self as guilt, where it is stored and hoarded, collected and valued as one's own.

The peculiar freedom which is expressed through self-possession or which expresses itself through the acquisition of a relationship of indebtedness to oneself alone is predicated on the assumption that it is possible to own oneself, that ownership is the authentic metaphor for identity. Max Stirner, in *The Ego and His Own*, most clearly articulated this basic assumption of the logic of behavior. Stirner argued that while the ancient Greeks found their ideal of identity in *arete* (the virtue of harmonious function) and the Renaissance found its ideal in the concept of *virtu* (strength, courage, heroic or manly action), modern man comprehended himself necessarily as *Eigentum* (property) (*Ego*, p. 237). Self-ownership (*Eigenheit*, "ownness") was for Stirner the basis of personality and was one's "whole being and existence":

> I am free from what I am *rid* of, owner of what I have in
> my *power* or what I control. *My own* I am at all times
> and under all circumstances, as I know how to have
> myself and do not throw myself away on others. (*Ego*,
> p. 206)

The assumption that freedom is self-possession is central to what I have called "the tradition of authenticity" in the history of modern Western political philosophy, the subject of Chapter 4 in this book.

The Political Psychology of Behavior

With its roots in Rousseau and Hegel, the tradition of authenticity responds to the basic facts of modern Western market society: the equation of price and worth, of property and identity. Most systematically articulated by Thomas Hobbes in the seventeenth century, these facts meant that, as Hobbes put it, a man's worth was his price, and therefore a thing dependent on others. This dependence was the source of the condition which Hobbes called the "estate of a desperate debtor," where despair involved the secret hatred which a person harbors toward someone who gives gifts which cannot be repaid (*Leviathan*, p. 81). The tradition of authenticity, I will argue, attempts to escape the estate of the desperate debtor by locating indebtedness within the self, by internalizing debt as the relationship of the self to itself, by taking the archaic legacy of danger, domination, and debt as one's own. This own it will call "guilt."

The location of indebtedness, reliance, dependence, freedom, power, and worth within an individual is the logical result of behavioral despair. We tend, today, to call this autonomy. What for the Greeks only could characterize a city (*polis*), namely the quality of self-governance (*autonomos*), comes in the modern West to define the person. The logic of behavior leads an individual to take within himself those attributes and relationships which traditionally had characterized community. Behavioral pathology, expressed, for example, by Louis Wolfson's attempt to completely possess a language of his own, reflects the culmination of the search for self-possession: to be a community unto oneself.

The location of autonomy within the self, of sovereignty within an individual, of legitimacy as an attribute of personal choice—in short, the taking within the self of the categories of public authority and political relationships—means that, as we hear more often, the personal is political. While our major institutions lose the attributes of the political (legitimacy and authority particularly), while the reality and "salience" of what most political scientists call "politics" is absent for an increasingly cynical people, a new "political" world flourishes within the self.

As early as 1955, Herbert Marcuse announced the need for a new narcissism to recover some space for the self in a world grown so systematically dominating that there was no room for privacy. Marcuse opened his preface to *Eros and Civilization* with this assertion:

> This essay employs psychological categories because they have become political categories. The traditional borderlines between psychology on the one side and political and social philosophy on the other have been made obsolete by the condition of man in the present era: formerly autonomous and identifiable psychical processes are being absorbed by the function of the individual in the state—by his public existence. . . . Psychology could be elaborated and practiced as a special discipline as long as the psyche could sustain itself against the public power, as long as privacy was real, really desired and self-shaped; if the individual has neither the ability nor the possibility to be for himself, the terms of psychology become the terms of the societal forces which define the psyche. (p. xvii)

But the ability to be "for oneself," far from being eroded in the present age, is precisely the culmination of the modern Western logic of behavior.

The collapse of the categories of psychology and politics is thus not to be understood here as a result of the state "absorbing" the individual, but rather as the result of the interiorization of the political. In fact, the consolidation of man for himself is far from being some utopian dream of self-actualization; human growth and the search for authenticity comprise an ongoing business in our times. Best-selling books record the progress of the new narcissism, teaching "How to be your own best friend," how to be real, how to be true to yourself, how to be here now. Hugh

Prather's *Notes to Myself* symbolizes the autobiographical character of the new narcissism, as does the growing literature of wom-
en's and men's liberation. The tone and character of this project
is best expressed for me in the best-selling title: "I ain't much,
baby, but I'm all I've got."

One contemporary student of political psychology has understood this narcissism implicitly and has attempted to formulate a
political theory totally based on what he calls "self-reference." He
argues that what we need is a "fresh conception" of ourselves in
America, a new conception of citizenship "exclusively in terms of
the individual." This conception entails the view that "our external public and otherwise visible lives take on the character of a
theater in which all of our *internal* lives are merely projected"
(Warren, *A Concept of Citizenship* . . .). That we can consider externality as a projection of our interiority means that there is
nothing "there" but what we put there. This proposition is idiocy.
The constitution which appears to matter for Bicentennial
America seems increasingly to be the "internal" constitution of
the self. To focus the political within the self-referential is a
symptom of behavioral despair.

Behavioral despair is an experience which touches the extremes
of both alienation and authenticity. There is an enormous literature in the modern West for which the most fundamental meaning
of alienation is the experience of not *owning* one's experience, the
experience of one's experience as other or alien. The "problem"
of alienation is, from this perspective, the problem of not being
one's own true self, and the "resolution" is in becoming one's
own, one's authentic self. Thus the problematic of alienation understood in this way is inseparable from the logic of ownership.
To know about alienation or authenticity, so understood, is the
privilege of the behavioral self. Such knowledge is unintelligible
apart from the way of knowing of the possessive unconscious. This
mode of knowing unites the meaning of both alienation and authenticity in one logic.

Take the example of the work of Erich Fromm. Fromm's basic
formulation of the problem of "alienated" man is that he ". . . is
owned by his own creation, and has lost ownership of himself."
For Fromm, to be alienated is to be a slave to "external" aims by
which the individual is "possessed" (*Sane*, pp. 114-115). Fromm's
understanding of this problem is itself an expression of the ideology of private possession. It is a "privileged" understanding in the
root of the word (*privilege* from *priva* + *lege*, private law). The law of

private possession is the ordering principle of the epistemological space within which the problem of alienation has its meaning.

In this sense, alienation is the dilemma of the behavioral self, for whom the logic of personality is inseparable from the logic of personalty, that is, from the law regulating private possessions (personal estate). The idea of personality as we understand it, as the attributes which are *one's own*, derives its logic from the fifteenth century law of personalty. The words *personality* and *personalty* are interchangeably used as meaning personal belongings in our legal tradition. In 1776, Blackstone commented

> Our courts now regard a man's personalty in a light
> nearly, if not quite, equal to his realty. (*Commentaries*,
> II, xxiv, 385)

That is to say that the American Revolution took place at a time in which private goods or possessions (capital or commodities) received legal recognition about equal to that of land (realty). The law of personalty is to personality as the law of realty is to reality. The question of whether a person is being "real" or not, whether he is his own person (not alienated), involves the interiorization of realty (and reality) within the person, the equating of personality and reality by collapsing the real into the personal, where the self is conceived of as the real thing, the thing-in-itself.

In a certain sense B. F. Skinner has understood this. *Beyond Freedom and Dignity* is the ideology which rejects the fetishism implicit in understanding personality as an inner possession, uncovering the Hobbesian conception which underlies our modern liberal overlay. But the Hobbesian framework lies beneath, not beyond, our world. Skinner's rejection of the idea of "autonomous man" is as if Hobbes had come alive again to refute, on the same old logic, Rousseau's criticism of his position. Skinner's criticism of the ideas of inner man returns to Hobbesian premises in order to consign sovereignty a place *outside* the individual as the determining otherness or environment where control is located.

This understanding is helpful in that it demystifies the ideology of interiority which is implicit in liberal-humanist views about the person. Thus it has been attacked predominantly from a moral standpoint by "humanist" psychologists. So it is important to see, as Skinner does, that autonomy cannot be located solely within the self, that it is always an involvement in otherness and that otherness is contextual. But Skinner does not perceive difference either, rather only the uniform regularities of environmental processes and controls, stripping the individual of agency, abolishing—like Hobbes—the illusion of free will.

The debate over the nature and value of autonomy which characterizes much of contemporary psychology can be seen as an argument from the two dichotomous extremes of the logic of behavior. Thus, for example, the contrast between Maslow and Skinner over the idea of autonomy poses Maslow's defense of self-actualization against Skinner's rejection of the assumption of self-possession. Maslow expressed the logic of self-actualization in this way:

> The self-actualizing individual, by definition gratified in his basic needs, is far less dependent, far less beholden, far more autonomous and self-directed than the deficiency-motivated man: . . . far from needing other people, growth-motivated people may actually be hampered by them. (*Psychology of Being*, p. 32)

[The idea that self-actualization may entail transcending need for others is central to the tradition of authenticity. See Chapter 4 in this book.]

Skinner replied to Maslow's proposition:

> C. S. Lewis put it bluntly: "Man is being abolished. . . ." What is being abolished is autonomous man—the inner man, the homunculus, the possessing demon, the man defended by the literature of freedom and dignity. ("Beyond Freedom and Dignity," prepublication)

Modern behavioral science, Skinner argues, should dis-possess us of the illusion of man the possessor, an illusion which he recognizes correctly as the ideal of liberal society and thinkers from Mill through Rousseau, or what he calls the "literature of freedom and dignity." In rejecting this literature, Skinner returns to Hobbes's conception of freedom, that "there can be no free subject, no free will, nor any *free*, but free from being hindered by opposition" (*Leviathan*, p. 43). Skinner's insights here are based on the Hobbesian confusion between world and marketplace. What Skinner understands is that worth and price are one, and he occasionally tries to demonstrate this etymologically: "The etymology of 'appreciate' is significant: to appreciate the behavior of a man is to put a price on it" (*Beyond*, p. 52). Thus Skinner criticizes the tendency of the literature of dignity to attribute "credit" to, or appreciate, an individual for what is inexplicable about his behavior. In its destruction of "mystery," modern behavioral science and technology strip away the mask of individual autonomy and demonstrate, Skinner says, that "nothing is eventually left for which autonomous man can take credit" (*Beyond*, p. 58). Since the inner man has been created, Skinner argues, in the image of the outer, a science of behavior shifts the credit back to the "environment," away from "internal" back to "external control." But external control has meant, since Hobbes, the control of demand in the marketplace; it is in struggle against this control that the literature of freedom and dignity has its meaning, in protest against the contingencies of the market. What Skinner offers is the systematization of external control, the removal of the obstacles to controlling behavior, the dis-possession of inner man. He would leave us with only one half of the logic of behavior, the logic of dis-possession; he does not speak to the despair of this position, which J. R. Robertson sang about in "Last of the Blacksmiths":

"Found Guilty," said the judge, "for not being in demand." (The Band, *Cahoots,* Capitol Records, Inc.)

For Maslow and the "humanist" psychologists, to be beyond the need of other people, to be able to distinguish between true (growth) needs and (deficiency-motivated) desires reflects the autonomy of the individual who chooses his acts in a self-referential way, who is not dominated by what people think or say, who is inner-directed, who is for himself, who responds to external demands, expectations, obligations with a shrug, and who will not be "beholden" to others. Such an individual is, in Nietzsche's title phrase, "Beyond Good and Evil," apparently as much freed from the custom character of morals as Skinner would have us be freed from the illusion of self-possession. But behavioral psychology is about possession—whether possessed by oneself or by one's environment, whether Maslow or Skinner.

What this debate signifies is a time of transition during which traditional cultural strictures against narcissism, against the sin of pride, are collapsing in the face of institutional decay. In this age, what I would call the "scripty" character of behavior is increasingly apparent and, depending upon which extreme of the logic of behavior is perceived, behavior appears either as potentially liberated from the constraints of custom or as determined by the operations of the environment. This alternative raises the possibility that we live in a time so dislocated, one in which a dominant cultural pattern is breaking down, that we cannot see clearly the process of dislocation.

The dramaturgical analogy to social existence—life as a game or a play—increasingly informs theoretical perspectives in many disciplines today. That we are only saying our lines, performing our parts in a drama scripted and patterned long before we were born, is a perspective common to role theory, game theory, Hannah Arendt's understanding of political activity, Erving Goffman's conception of the presentation of self in everyday life, and Eric Berne's theory of transactional analysis. Any perspective which claims the ability to isolate the "games people play" or the "scripts people live" presupposes the possibility of distancing oneself from the rules, norms, and expectations of one's situation. It is the very "givenness" of our culture, its custom character, which, when expressed or performed unselfconsciously or uncritically, leads us to characterize behavior as "scripty," an individual as not "real," not autonomous, or not authentic.

Having employed these terms from the vocabulary of transactional analysis, I offer a brief discussion (based largely on the perspective of Steiner's *Scripts*) of this approach to the enterprise of living.

What is observed in these dramaturgical analogies is an individual as his culture writ small, and the experience is often jarring to an acute observer, giving the impression that the person is somehow trapped in a "movie" which is happening to him, playing a scene as his parents would have done it, somehow "not there" where he is. In our time, when the moral and customary patterns of legitimate behavior in many sacred institutions (the presidency, for one) have lost their halo, the existence of scripty or "inauthentic" behavior in an individual appears to be a central aspect of the oppressiveness of life, a form of abuse which comes closer to what we mean by *repression* than to traditional understandings of *oppression*. Thus the perception of an individual performing a script presupposes the "internalization of man," the increasing inability to locate external oppression or domination, where the wisdom of Pogo comes to express the feeling that whatever it is, we do it to ourselves: "We have met the enemy and he is us." The internalization of domination, the idea that each of us is his own most dangerous enemy, is the prerequisite of our attempts to become our own best friends: "We are accountable only to ourselves for what happens to us in our lives" (Newman and Berkowitz, *Best Friend*, p. 22).

The internalization of accountability and recognition ("It is up to us [as individuals] to give ourselves recognition.") gives us the internal "economics" of the behavioral self, expressed in what transactional analysis has called the "stroke economy" ("stroke" being its unit of recognition), based on the assumption that human identity and worth are scarce goods. To genuinely recognize the identity of another, to accept difference and dependence and need as categories of experience is to be vulnerable in a context of scarcity and competition (where worth is price). What I would call the "self-possession script" is an attempt to deal with the condition which Hobbes thought was natural to mankind, what he termed "universal vulnerability." It is through this script that people are taught how to become invulnerable and successful in manipulating the stroke economy by avoiding commitment, dependence, and need. The "rational man" of the stroke economy maximizes his credit, collects what Eric Berne called "trading stamps," the enduring emotions which are stored up within us because they are not acted out (anger and guilt particularly). Enduring emotions (which are saved) are held onto and endure beyond the events which cause them. The emotions of the self-possessed individual are bottled up, stored up, saved, the interior capital of the market economy of the psyche, the substance of behavioral despair.

But to locate all meaning within, to withdraw the locus of life into the self, implies an enormous dislocation of the person from his situation and his past, the situation of the self "at-a-loss," threatened by some Skinnerian nightmare of an engulfing external world, tempted to withdraw into some Maslowian idiocy. This condition I have termed the situation of *extasis* or what might be called the alienation of the behavioral self. Expressions of this experience are widespread in the contemporary world. This is what they sound like:

> No, sir. You have to pull yourself out of it, otherwise all that's happening is that our society is swallowing you up. . . . It's all so pitiful. I feel dead inside. Lifeless, burdened, desperate. Not really lifeless. I don't know. There's nothing to do really. (Quoted in Cottle, *The Sexual Revolution* . . .)

Fritz Perls, the originator of gestalt therapy, articulated a "prayer" which expresses the wisdom and the madness of the logic of behavioral despair:

> I do my thing, and you do your thing.
> I am not in this world to live up to your
>   expectations
> And you are not in this world to live up to mine.
> You are you, and I am I,
> And if by chance, we find each other, it's beautiful.
> If not, it can't be helped. (*Gestalt*, p. 4)

Though I believe there is a deeply important truth in this prayer, it is partial, the wisdom of idiocy. That the wisdom of the logic of behavior culminates in idiocy exemplifies the process whereby the norms of a culture are illuminated by its pathology. The possibility of autonomous man, in other words, has been a necessity for us. That we are like only to ourselves, related by chance, liberated from the expectations of others is a *description* of the dissociation and dislocation of our age, about which the Hebrew prophet Hillel lamented:

> If I am not for myself, who will be for me?
> And if not now, when?
> And if I am only for myself,
> What am I?

2
Extasis: The Context of Behavior

That to be oneself is to be one's own has become a basic principle of identification in the modern West. This principle is the pattern of coherence which constitutes a way of thinking about ourselves, the axioms, the deductive connections, and the logical compatibilities that define the context of meaning within which it is possible to be and possess (or not to be and to lose) one's self.

Oscar Wilde once commented that as the motto "Know thyself" characterized the ancient world, so "Be thyself" would be written over the portal of modernity. But the self which was known in antiquity differs significantly from the self which is its own. What we understand as self-consciousness and what the Greeks called self-knowledge (*sophrosune*) are distanced by the assumptions of subjectivity which characterize our experiences of identity and identification.

To speak convincingly to the question of the characteristic "modernity" of the assumptions of the possessive unconscious would involve distinguishing classical and modern conceptions of self-consciousness, self-knowledge, and self-possession. This is beyond the scope of this book. It is clear, for example, that a possessive metaphor for knowing is present in Plato's *Theatetus* (where "having" knowledge is distinguished from "possessing" it and the mind is compared to an aviary where facts are kept secure even if not always readily accessible). Self-knowledge is a different matter, however. The Platonic understanding is that self-knowledge takes place only within a political context, in terms of the necessary relationship between man and *polis*. Stanley Rosen (in "Sophrosune and Selbstbewusstsein") argues that there is a central distinction between the Platonic notion of self-knowledge and the Hegelian conception of self-consciousness. Hegel himself maintained that the Greeks lacked the recognition of the principle of subjectivity and he roots this recognition (as I do as well in Chapter 3) in the Reformation.

Generally, classical and Renaissance conceptions of identity, articulated in terms of the conceptions of *arete* and *virtu* respectively, emphasize relational dimensions of human experience and contrast significantly, I believe, with the essentially depoliticized expression of identity (which can be taken away by others) which is the subject of this book.

This self which we know as a separation from others is known in the mode of deprivation or private possession. Where human identity is defined by subjectivity, inwardness, or interiority, the experience of being deprived of intimate and enduring associations and relationships with others is discounted and is transformed into the meaning of freedom. This is the freedom and privilege of the *bourgeois* individual, fearfully suspicious that others will deprive him of his possessions, including himself. To conceive of the self as a "thing-in-itself," *basically* and essentially separate from others who threaten to "alienate" what is one's own, is possible only where the structure of social relationships and the corresponding mode of economic production are the organization of private possession. To be able to think of oneself as "living property" means that the logic of socioeconomic relationships has penetrated the psyche, that our self-conceptions are produced by the internalization of the root metaphors of possession and ownership. Subjectivity understood in this way is intelligible in terms of private property, as a hidden, private relationship: the self's ownership of itself.

Conceptions of human identity, like conceptions of "human nature," are always social in the sense in which they express the shared (that is, social) patterns of assumptions about the value and meaning of a given context. The conception of the self as its own entails, therefore, a contradiction: that what we share is our separation and our privacy. It is true, I think, that people always are what they share and how they associate. But this truth is obscured within the epistemological space of idiocy, where people share and associate largely in private. To identify oneself as, say, a citizen, a craftsman, or a woman would be to make explicit the activities and relationships which define these identities. So, too, the mode of identity of idiocy reveals the social logic which is its meaning: the logic of behavior. The mirror of idiocy reflects the logic of this social relationship.

The definition of the self given by Søren Kierkegaard in the middle of the nineteenth century is the paradigmatic example of this mode. The Kierkegaardian definition of the self as that relation which "relates itself to its own self" (*Sickness*, p. 146) locates the relational quality of all identity processes within the self. Inner-relatedness, the ability (problem, value) of "being at one with onself" locates relatedness within the self. To be with oneself, beside oneself, outside oneself presupposes that the self is basically social and can be conceived as such, on the model of relationships with others. But this relational character of identity becomes obscured because it is *self*-contained. When the meaning of one's existence can be said to come from within the self because it is basically a private affair, the fact that all meaning is social and that the separate private self reflects a context of privacy and relationships of separation is obscured. That I can be my own is the application of private law (or privilege) to human identity. We are a privileged people to the extent to which we seek to be free from indebtedness to others. Authenticity is the privilege of idiocy, the private law of the behavioral self. Self-possession, the owning of oneself, is the socioeconomic content of subjectivity in the context of idiocy.

Theodor Adorno has shown that the consequence of German Existentialism, which desocietalizes human subjectivity into an "in-itself," is to transform "a bad empirical reality into a transcendence." Philosophy, therefore, "no longer has to bother about the societal and natural-historical origin of this title deed which declares that the individual owns himself." Adorno understood that authenticity had become a "jargon," an aura in a context in which the individual "who himself can no longer rely on any firm possession, holds onto himself in his extreme abstractness as the last, the supposedly unlosable possession" (*Jargon*, p. 116). But this "abstractness," the genesis of which I will explore below, is the analogue, the symbolization, of actual social relationships. It reveals a political theory, a theory of the basic assumptions that structure our collective lives and are represented in the ways in which we think about ourselves. This way of thinking was described by Merleau-Ponty in these words:

> If it is perfect, the contact of my thought with itself seals
> me within myself, and prevents me from ever feeling
> that anything eludes my grasp; there is no opening, no
> "aspiration" towards another for this self of mine, which
> constructs the totality of being and its own presence in
> the world, which is defined in terms of self-possession,
> and which never finds anything outside itself but what it
> has put there. (*Perception*, p. 373)

[This passage sums up Merleau-Ponty's interpretation of the Cartesian doctrine of the *Cogito*.]

Never to find anything in the world except what you have put there means that the world has become a projection of the self, or that the self has become a world unto itself. To be responsible for one's own presence in the world, to attempt to really *be* where one is, is to complete the world within the self. To "make the world" (the motto over Walt Whitman's writing desk) is a conception possible only for the consciousness which knows no boundary or mediation between itself and the world. That the world is made up, that it *is*, as Berkeley said, *because* we perceive it, is conceivable only where it is possible to understand that meaning and value are given to the "world," which therefore is not a thing in itself, but rather a result of our work. Where the world is not "given" to us as valuable but rather has value to the extent to which we produce it, this value is a result of "mixing" the world and the self, making the world one's own.

To make the world one's own, to mix yourself with the world, is for both Locke and Marx the labor theory of value. To explicitly recognize that identity, the "self," is made up, to see the self as a work of art (life as art), to make the world and oneself one's own is to posit the self as the locus of all value. That work can be seen as a relationship of the self to itself means that the work ethos has become *self*-conscious. We have thus come to a point where we can understand Marx's statement that people produce *themselves* through their productive activity: we can recognize that we are what we make of ourselves. To self-consciously work on ourselves is to make human identity the object of our labor, to make the self one's own product.

Idiocy is the internalization of human identity, whether expressed in John Stuart Mill's conception of self-development or Maslow's idea of self-actualization, the psychology of inner-directedness, or the philosophy of authenticity. The imperialist project of completing the world within the self is the most highly individuated form of the labor theory of value. Only where the self is one's own product can the self be one's own property.

The Political Epistemology of Self-Fetishism

Consider this image:

> Captain Crunch took his name from the cereal box which
> contained a whistle which exactly duplicated the tonal
> frequency which the Bell System uses to register the fact
> that a phone call has been made, but not connected.
> Blow the whistle into the phone after receiving a call

and you can talk forever for nothing. Before he was arrested, Captain Crunch traveled around the U.S., alone, in his V.W. bus, making illegal phone calls. His most famous call was placed from one phone in the bus, completely around the world, to another phone next to him. The phone rang and he picked it up. When asked what he said to himself when he was connected with himself around the world, he replied that he said, first into one phone and then into the other: "Hello." (Rosenbaum, "Secrets of the Little Blue Box")

The image of Captain Crunch expresses a particular way of living in the world without being at home in it. These lines from a song popular in the 1950s capture the freedom of Captain Crunch:

I am free and I'm happy to be free;
to be free in the way I want to be.
But once in a while when I'm talking to myself,
and there's no one there to disagree,
I look up and I cry to a big empty sky,
won't there ever be a home for me?

The freedom of Captain Crunch is a self-possessed freedom, the freedom of the solipsistic conversation with oneself. What one says to oneself, the internal dialogue which we carry around within us, appears to be totally within the control of the individual. As such, any "power" over what we say to ourselves refers to a project which promises a freedom not contingent or dependent on other people: the project to be oneself.

The truth of Captain Crunch is that "Hello" is as far as the conversation of the self with itself can go. Where the "external" world is so abstract that the self, totally isolated, can encompass it, can even conceive of the project of calling itself around the world on the telephone, then there is no content, no meaning to its acts except the content or meaning which is its own.

We live in a time in which the self has become a fetish, a thing-in-itself. When there is nothing else to rely on, when we are afraid, alone, depressed, the one thing we increasingly count on is ourselves. I am the reliable thing, the dependable, responsible, individual (undividable) thing, the thing to invoke when all else fails. I mediate my own experience; only I stand between myself and meaninglessness. I am the sane, wise, and true thing. Thus speaks self-fetishism.

Søren Kierkegaard first formulated the epistemological principle of self-fetishism, that truth is subjectivity and that the self, that which relates itself to itself (or says hello to itself) can be true (or false, or falsely conscious of itself). Self-fetishism has informed our most basic assumptions about what we know and how we know it.

Truth, from the self-fetishistic perspective, is inwardness, or as Kierkegaard expressed it:

> An objective uncertainty held fast in an appropriation
> process of the most passionate inwardness is the truth,
> the highest truth for an existing individual. (*Postscript*,
> p. 182)

Such truth, Kierkegaard said, involved the passion of the infinite. He meant this in the religious sense that the ultimate truth for a Christian believer is the truth of the infinite. But in this statement a broader insight is implicit: that there is no content to the infinite, that the search for inwardness as truth is an infinite project, since to find "it" is by definition impossible. "It" is whatever I am when I am true to myself. The truth of inwardness is infinite because it cannot be falsified. Thus Kierkegaard says:

> It is the passion of the infinite that is the decisive factor,
> and not its content, for its content is precisely itself.
> (*Postscript*, p. 181)

Thus the true self, which can lose itself and hence be false or at-a-loss, can stand as its own criterion of meaning and value, so long as it is "true to itself." To be able to claim that I am "true to myself" means that our most basic epistemological category, truth, is located within the interior of the individual. That the self is irreducible and unmediated, that it is given in our experience as the very principle of intelligibility of our experience, reflects the depth of our self-fetishistic assumptions.

Those assumptions which are unquestioned or indubitable provide the necessary ground for our knowing anything. This ground of assumption is itself a kind of knowing which lets life go on, lets us proceed: it is the rule of our procedures, that sort of knowing which we have by virtue of our context or condition. What we know *about*—the objects, images, and ideas to which we pay attention, in which we invest meaning—is organized by the mode of our contextual knowing. The formal rules, the metaphors and models which govern the objects of our thinking, refer us to the basic givens of our experience. That attention can be "paid," that meaning can be "invested," that we can, in other words, conceptualize the activities of looking and caring through metaphors of commodity capitalism, are examples of the context character of our consciousness.

This difference between what we know about and how we know it parallels the distinction which Michel Foucault has drawn between *connaissance* and *savoir*. By *connaissance* he means the relationship between a given subject-matter (such as political psychology) and an object of knowledge (such as the "self") together with the formal rules which govern this relationship. That political identity refers to the "self," and that it is an object of disinterested scholarship by professional political scientists are examples of this kind of knowing. To then ask the question "What are the assumptions which make this knowledge possible?" is to explore the contextual basis of our knowing. For Foucault, to ask this question is to attempt to understand our *savoir*, the "conditions which are necessary in a particular period for this or that type of object to be given *connaissance*, and for this or that enunciation to be formulated" (*Archeology*, p. 15).

The uncovering of the *savoir* of self-fetishism, of what makes it possible to know in the mode of the "true to oneself," is an exercise in what I would call political epistemology. That mode of knowing which permits us to know some things in certain ways and not others is the depth-political order of our lives. It is my argument here that the *savoir* of self-fetishism is the condition of *extasis*. *Extasis* is that condition of basic dissociation, privacy, and social isolation wherein meaning, value, and truth come to be located within the individual. *Extasis* is the mode of *savoir* which denies the basic principle of contextual knowing, a form of social order which denies sociality, the context of dislocation as a way of life.

The experience of contextlessness, of being distanced and estranged from one's circumstances, was what the Greeks called *ekstasis* (out-of-place). *Stasis* was one of those dialectical Greek words which meant both itself and its opposite. When contrasted with *kinesis* (motion) it meant stability and continuity; when contrasted with *ekstasis*, however, *stasis* meant just the opposite: being at odds with, at variance, or as applied to a *polis*, being distracted by civil, especially economic, strife. To be beyond the distraction of economic conflict was to be *ekstatic*, and here *ekstasis* signified withdrawal of the soul into a mystic or prophetic trance, but also insanity and bewilderment. This sense of *ekstasis* was preserved in the medieval *alienatio mentis* or *extasis* (mental alienation, withdrawal, loss, derangement), and it is the root of our word *alienation*. (See Rotenstreich, "On the Ecstatic Sources of the Concept of 'Alienation.' ")

I have gone back to the root of *alienation* to emphasize that the experience of being out of place, of not being located in a context, is the experience of idiocy. To be for oneself alone, a private and separate person, is to be in *extasis*. There is where the behavioral self, which knows itself through itself, is. But we cannot say "where it is *located*," since its principle of location is dislocation, as its principle of association is dissociative. To the extent to which "behavior" expresses a habitual, recurrent, or "normal" pattern of experience, then distraction, withdrawal, bewilderment, and idiocy are the most stable and continuous aspects of our lives.

It is this static sense of *behavior* which we most often invoke when we speak of behavioral laws or regularities. But this use suggests that for the modern West our "behavioral" norms express the routinization of idiocy. Thus *stasis* for modernity entails the predictable set of expectations whereby identity and property are equated, where withdrawal and self-possessed idiocy are not philosophical positions but rather ways of life, where *ekstasis* is *stasis*.

Ekstasis, ecstatic contemplation or vision, was for the Greeks the privilege of the philosopher, of the few. In our time this privilege has been generalized: we are all philosophers. The condition of Captain Crunch, the exstatic contemplation of an abstract universe as a whole, unmediated by concrete tensions and conflicts with others, is the context in which philosophy is abolished because it is realized in our daily lives. We are expected to be idiots.

Yet we do not generally see that to be expected not to consider the expectations of others is an expectation. The project to "be yourself" is thus a social project, intelligible as the *savoir* of the behavioral self. To be one's own true self is to be*have* oneself: it is a normal, not an exceptional thing to do. Thus I employ the word *extasis* to define the context of the behavioral self, whose only proper alternatives are about possession.

To understand that human identity is mediated by relations with others demands perceiving that the self is social, dependent upon mutuality and reciprocity. But the epistemological ordering of self-fetishism collapses the experience of our sociality into the need to hold onto oneself at all costs. This transforms mutuality into competition for scarce goods. Reciprocity becomes the pattern of contractual obligations which defines responsibility as accountability, reason as cost-benefit analysis, in a context which is seen as basically dissociated. As C. B. MacPherson has pointed out, this conception reflects, in fact, a particular form of society (the possessive market society), organized around the logic of what he calls possessive individualism. MacPherson points out that

> the possessive character of individualism in the 17th Century was found in its conception of the individual as essentially the proprietor of his own person or capacities, owing nothing to society for them. The individual was seen neither as a moral whole, nor as a part of a larger social whole, but as an owner of himself. The relation of ownership, having become for more and more men the critically important relation determining their actual freedom . . . was read back into the nature of the individual. The individual, it was thought, is free inasmuch as he is proprietor of his person and capacities. The human essence is freedom from dependence on the wills of others, and freedom is a function of possession. (*Possessive Individualism*, p. 3)

Material possession was the existential ground of freedom in the seventeenth century. Today it is no longer so. The increasing dependence of all persons upon large organizational units for employment and welfare is the contemporary ground of economic freedom. (See the literature of "post-industrialism": Bell, *Post-Industrial*; Fuchs, *Service*.) Yet the ideology of market society still endures—the dead hand of history which preserves the idiocy of the sovereign individual as the truest, best, most free thing. Today we call it authenticity, the individual as a moral whole. This view is the most sophisticated development of the logic of *extasis*, the most perverse expression of the *savoir* which is about possession.

To the extent to which we experience our identities and the ways in which we identify others through this way of knowing, our context appears to be that of an aggregation of idiots. But this presses the very limits of what we mean by a context or condition. (Our word *context* is a work word derived from the now obsolete verb *to contex*, which meant to weave together, to form by the interweaving of parts. The words *text*, *textile*, and *texture* are from the same root. Written texts have a texture, a structure of words woven together and forming a context of meaning—and out of context the words mean nothing, or something else.) A context is not the sum of its parts but their ordering principle of intelligibility and meaning. The context, or epistemological space, which I am describing has idiocy as its ordering principle. Hence only within such a space can we think of the individual as a context unto himself, or the part as the whole.

Thus the interiorization of meaning, the idiosyncratization of value and truth and the ability to think of autonomy as an attribute of the self, mystifies our perception of context. Situations in which idiocy is the ordering principle are in fact progressively desituating. The inner-migration of contextual meaning implies that what is shared becomes less clear and more abstract. In the situation of being desituated, the integration of person and context can take place only within a self so fetishized and imperial that it can possess truth as *its own*.

This conception of the "true to oneself" is basically the logic of egoistic appropriation translated into epistemological terms. Hegel, in *The Phenomenology of Mind*, succinctly characterized the epistemological space wherein truth is conceived in a fundamentally possessive way, where the truth of an object

> . . . lies in the object as my (*meinem*) object, or lies in
> the "meaning" (*Meinen*), in what I "mean"; it is because
> *I* know it. (*Mind*, p. 153)

Lionel Rubinoff (in "The Dialectic of Work and Labour") has pointed to this passage as indicating that ". . . to perceive the object as mine is synonymous with perceiving the object as having meaning" (p. 165). He goes on to conclude that "implicit in the very act of perception" is the "notion that I can be secure only about that which I possess for myself," that the world "is my will, my idea and my property." Though he suggests that perhaps "in the attempt to take hold of the world we tend also to falsify it," he roots this falsification in what he calls "the curse" or the burden of "fallen" man who must seek redemption by possessing the world. In this Rubinoff comes close to Sartre's notion that possession is expressive of the project to become God. See p. 115 of this book.

To the extent that we see encounters with other people as the loss of our freedom and meaning, we begin to reify what is shared and to project it into an abstraction which we call "society," from which we attempt to extricate ourselves, with respect to which we stand "at-a-loss." Society becomes the symbol of all that threatens the loss of our private, interior meaning and control. If the only truth is *my* truth, I must learn to hide myself from others, to withdraw as far into *my* idiocy as is possible. In order to believe that we are all idiots, we must hide from one another the fact that it is precisely this belief which we share.

Thus we are woven together so as not to see the interweaving. The text and the texture of our lives are the dreams of idiots, where, in Bob Dylan's words, "everybody sees himself walking around with no one else." But the deepest dreams of our idiocy are themselves shared, our most private fears are also public, not idiosyncratic, though we have so deeply repressed our social intelligence that these fears are unconscious. In such a context it is a political act to offer Dylan's response to the idiot's dream: "I'll let you be in my dream if I can be in yours." All is the same from within the idiot's dream: the world is not differentiated. I "know" that you are an idiot because I "know" that I must be alone, my own. Undifferentiated otherness, abstract conceptions of association, and the basic rule of being "true to oneself" characterize the context of our idiocy.

Extasis is, then, a condition of monotonous boredom and powerlessness expressed in the way in which we use the word *society* in the sense of "them" or "the system"—as an external reification of the principle of association and agency. When we say of the "society" that it does things, we are making the principle of our association into a mechanism which operates "out there" and at a distance from us.

The radical separation of self-consciousness from society means that detachment, invulnerability, indifference, and independence come to characterize the ways in which we relate to the world around us. Thus Saul Bellow describes the boredom of everyday life:

> For me the self-conscious ego is the seat of boredom. This increasing, swelling, domineering, painful self-consciousness is the only rival of the political and social powers that run my life (business, technological-bureaucratic powers, the state). You have a great organized movement of life, and you have the single self, independently conscious, proud of its detachment and its absolute immunity, its stability and its power to remain unaffected by anything whatsoever—by the sufferings of others or by society or by politics or external chaos. ("On Boredom," p. 22)

This grotesquely enlarged self-consciousness rivals the powers of its corporate organizational environment through the power "to remain unaffected by anything whatsoever." But this "power" is really only an inflated impotence. As Adorno has put it:

> The weaker the individual becomes, from a societal
> perspective, the less can he become calmly aware of his
> own impotence. He has to puff himself up into selfness,
> in the way the futility of this selfness sets itself up as
> what is authentic, as Being. (*Jargon*, p. 293)

The everyday indifference and boredom which Bellow characterizes is structured through the experience of futility, is the transformation of impotence and isolation into strength. It parallels precisely the philosophical transformation of idiocy into authenticity. Consider the experience of watching the evening news with Walter Cronkite or his counterpart: we are witness to world monetary, energy, and legitimacy crises as if they were spectacles which happen to us, which are presented to us as coming from "out there." (I once watched a battalion of United States Marines shot down, live, in Hue, Vietnam, while I ate and apparently digested a chicken dinner.) The meaning of *crisis*—that is, an important development or "turning point" which can be clearly discriminated and which is decisive for better or worse—is lost in the monotony of undifferentiated abstractions. Today *crisis* means "suspense"—the question "How will they get out of it?," whether asked about one's favorite football team or the machinations of the president's men.

The experience of boundless pride and self-license, of the man who loved only in order to intensify his own self-assertion, was what Dostoyevsky called "idiotism." In his notebooks for *The Idiot*, he wrote that he was trying to depict "the domination of [one]self out of pride (not morality)." But for us, self-domination has come to be an aspect of our mores; idiotism is the conquest "in here" in the face of the perceived chaos "out there," an expression of power within powerlessness.

Our view of experience as abstract externality, as that which "happens" to us, has come to characterize in the modern West an epochal sense of discontinuity. It is in this sense that ours has been called the "accidental century" (Harrington, *Accidental*), discontinuous with its past, out of place in the scheme of history. In *The Possessed*, Dostoyevsky presented a picture of this discontinuity as insanity, murder, arson, and suicide, and remarked that "what worried everyone was the impossibility of discovering a connecting link in the chaos." In the face of this perceived impossibility, crisis and chaos begin to be appreciated for their own sake and any happening which elicits a heightened sense of the happenstance character of life reinforces this perspective. Dostoyevsky described an expedition of young people who discover that a man has committed suicide in a hotel. The idea is presented that everyone go in and *observe* the suicide. One of the group comments: "Everything's so boring, one can't be squeamish over one's amusements, so long as they're interesting" (*Possessed*, p. 332).

But the situation within which the experience of the world as accidental chaos is raised to aesthetic proportions is that of *extasis*. Any *ekstasis* (philosophical withdrawal) fails in its attempt to gain perspective on this situation since it merely is symptomatic of the situation itself. Thus one of the traditional roles of the political philosopher, the reevaluation of an ongoing *statis* with an end to reestablish an older or envision an alternative form of *stasis*, is unsuited to the demands on political philosophy in the situation of *extasis*, where withdrawal *is* the ongoing *stasis*. Thus, for example, Machiavelli's concern to establish "lo stato" (from *stare*, *statum*, to stand), a stable and predictable order (*Discourses*, Bk. I, Ch. 6), appears today to be a redundant or meaningless concern: history, many tell us, has ended; ideology is over, action is superfluous. Better to withdraw and contemplate the chaos, the boredom, of the end of history (Hegel's term) which is *happening to us*.

If *extasis* is the situation within which we find ourselves, if the categories of the "happening" or the "accidental" reflect our tendencies to fetishize the self cut off from meaningful connection with the world, then it would appear that a significant task of contemporary political philosophy is, to draw on Nietzsche, the "redemption of accidents": the articulation of the meaning of *extasis*. It must also speak to the despair of the End of History, must make that despair intelligible. Political philosophy today can begin this task by making articulate the historical development and philosophical assumptions of the self "at-a-loss."

We are today like those people whom Plato described in his allegory of the cave: chained so that we cannot see one another, watching images which pass before us, reflections of events the origins of which we do not know. Plato wrote that in such a situation in which there was no understanding of how people and events were connected, prizes would be given to those who could predict the pattern of events, who could guess which image or illusion would come next. We have a name for people who predict the patterns of what Jacques Ellul calls our "political illusions," those facts which happen to people but are not shaped by them: scientists. Most political science presupposes the routinization of idiocy, the experience of politics as that which happens out there. Thus the studies of the regularities of "political behavior" replicate the passivity, apathy, cynicism, and boredom which constitute the *extasis* of our everyday lives. It should be clear that if political science is the science of what happens "out there" and if idiocy is the experience of the self separate from what is political, then the two belong together and are mutually reinforcing abstractions. My concern in this book is to demonstrate the "out there in here," by questioning the meaning of the term *political behavior* as it is commonly employed. This term roughly translated means for me: the dilemmas of people in an idiotic context as they react to what is happening to them. In other words, political behavior as we dominantly understand it is boredom.

Extasis and the Problem of Boredom

In classical Freudian terms, boredom refers to the experience, in the individual, of simultaneous need for intense activity and lack of incitement to act. This tension has been described as not knowing "how one ought or wants to be active" (Fenichel, *Collected Papers*, p. 292). The absence of instinctual incitement is presumed to lead to the search for stimulation from the outside world, necessary because instincts to act have been repressed. Fenichel draws the analogy to someone who has "forgotten a name and inquires about it from others" (*Collected Papers*, p. 293). To the extent to which the forgotten name is one's own, we might say that the individual does not know who he is and enlists others in the search. This turn toward the "external" world to achieve a sense of oneself demands that externality be constantly stimulating. But such an expectation is doomed to fail, doomed to discover in the world only the monotony of disappointed hopes. As the external world does not sufficiently excite, the individual withdraws his libido from it: he sleeps. The monotony he discovers becomes a soporific, as, for example, the monotony of praying is a form of intoxication or ecstasy.

The alternatives for the self involved in this conflict are either withdrawal or ecstasy, alternative forms of being out-of-place (*ecstasy* from *ekstasis*): both in withdrawal and in intoxication the self is not at home, with its world or with itself. Being out-of-place is expressed sexually in the absence of differentiation between sexual excitation and gratification. Excitation itself, rather than an existing person (who offers potential gratification), is the focus of interest for the self. This is the sexual manifestation of "self-fetishism." Fenichel describes this activity as intoxication (to create a sense of self-respect) plus the instinct for wandering (the urge toward distraction) (*Collected Papers*, pp. 299-300).

If we abstract from this framework the characteristics of boredom—not knowing how one ought to act or wants to act, not knowing who one is, confusion between excitation and gratification, the absence of mediation, and the characteristic experiences of intoxication, withdrawal, and wandering (what I have called *extasis*)—we are faced with the existential attitude which Nietzsche saw as the advent of modern nihilism. At the cultural level, these characteristics of being out-of-place represented for Nietzsche a nomadic or homeless wandering, the absence of what he called a "mythical home" (*Tragedy*, #23, p. 136). To raise in this way the problem of boredom in terms of cultural identity is to ask what the world must be like for boredom to be possible. This is to focus on the "situation" of *extasis*, to search to locate the historical context within which the problem of boredom emerges.

It is my contention that, for modernity, the situation of *extasis* is that context of ambiguity which Hegel described as masters without slaves and slaves without masters, and that it is a permanent possibility for the behavioral self. It is a situation which represents the void which looms beyond the horizon of meaning of the possessive unconscious and which also represents the realm of compensatory experiences (intoxication and wandering) which perpetuate resignation to those limits. Most positively expressed it is the situation of being "masterless"; and, as we shall see in Chapter 3, in some ways the idea of "masterless men" can be taken as a metaphor for modernity. Yet what is most significant about the rise of the modern behavioral self is that it *relates to itself* as master to slave. Thus the self as property both dominates and submits to itself and is situated to the extent to which it can hold onto itself. Experiences beyond the logic of possession imply the loss of self, the inability to calculate that which is appropriate, the inability to be situated along the dimension of possessive possibilities. Another way of saying this is: to the degree to which being situated reflects the limits of our history, the situation of *extasis* reflects being cut off from history (to use the Hegelian terms, the end of history). This experience has been described, accurately I think, as that in which "the individual has become more introspective, the society . . . increasingly more abstract and remote" (Strong, "Hold Onto Your Brains," p. 347).

The crucial experience of such a world—regardless of whether its parameters are seen in terms of leisure, immediate gratification, or the end of history—is the experience of boredom. This experience manifests itself in a special aesthetic, preoccupied with questions of style and personal purity. It is this aesthetic which Kierkegaard first represented as a form of "social prudence," designed to cope with the realization that boredom is the root of all evil.

There was an aesthetic response to boredom which Kierkegaard called "The Rotation Method," which, because it emphasized the arbitrary and accidental in existence, could cope with despair where systematic theory and escape could not. This aesthetic closely parallels those contemporary attempts at defining identity in "protean" terms.

See R. J. Lifton, *Boundaries*, section 4. The idea of "protean" identity refers to that self which is beset by "endless partial alternatives" and has no clear boundaries. The protean self-process is, for Lifton, not pathological as such. He suggests that it may be one of the functional patterns necessary "to life in our times" (p. 44). I would suggest that the whole question of pathology be understood in the context of the historical development of the behavioral self, and that from this perspective the protean self is the logical conclusion of this process, the culmination of that framework of meaning which equates both freedom and power with self-possession.

Because it can be produced only by the self which has defined itself in terms of property, this aesthetic deserves close attention. The point of it is to live life intensively, to raise to an absolute the character of the accidental. Since, as Kierkegaard said, the "arbitrariness in oneself corresponds to the accidental in the external world," to relate the internal "concrete-arbitrary" (the individual out-of-place) to the external "abstract-accidental" (history, politics, society) is to provide coherence to the situation of *extasis*. The attempt to relate the concrete-arbitrary to the abstract-accidental (the individual to society) is central to what I refer to in Chapter 3 as the "logic of abstraction"; it is expressed in the need to do everything at once, to relate two abstractions simultaneously, to bridge the gap of estrangement between concrete individuals through an act which ties the isolated, behavioral self to "everybody," to an abstract totality. Examples of this attempt are common:

> I need one shot. One crumby lousy shot in the dark. Just
> loud enough for everybody to hear. (Quoted in Cottle,
> "The Sexual Revolution . . .")

The lived experience of the separation of the individual from history and society is reflected in the aesthetic choice which one makes to perceivé the world as externality and accident. One makes this choice to save one from boredom, from the emptiness of a world which has "absorbed" the individual and his uniqueness. From this point of view the problem of boredom can be understood as the absence of differentiation in the face of the massness of modern society, its bureaucratic routine and the similarity of functions which it demands of its members: a world without difference.

From this perspective the self is seen as faced with options which are identical, with "infinite possibilities" each of which is arbitrary and which, from the aesthetic point of view, present the individual with the option "Either/Or, you will regret both." If this is the meaning of choice, if it's all nothing (*tout n'est rien*), the aesthetic response to this situation is to focus on the accidental as the expression of that identity. Life becomes a dreamlike projection of any arbitrary potential of the self onto any accidental quality of its surroundings, an idiot's dream. If all existence is the repetition of this pattern, then all choice is resignation. All that matters is style. In this manner Kierkegaard described the way in which one copes with, even comes to appreciate, a boring lecturer who happens also to sweat profusely while he lectures: by intensively focusing (arbitrarily) on the drop of sweat on the end of his nose. This is the character of the accidental: any imaginative association can be arbitrarily projected onto an undifferentiated reality. The attractiveness of the idea of externality (or history) as an accident is that it allows the self in *extasis* to resign itself to an ethic of withdrawal and the inability to act, while simultaneously achieving a "sense" of participation with its surroundings, a feeling of efficacy or power.

In his essay on "Heidegger's Analytic and Its Meaning for Psychiatry," Ludwig Binswanger argued that only those who in Kierkegaard's terms are "at odds with the fundamental conditions of existence" can be "neurotic," whereas only he who " 'knows' of the unfreedom of finite human existence and who obtains 'power' over his existence within his very powerlessness is unneurotic or 'free.' " He condludes that the sole task of psychotherapy lies in "assisting man toward this 'power' " (p. 218). This "power within powerlessness" is, I think, based on resignation to possessive limits of meaning (projected into "fundamental conditions") and is synonymous with self-possession.

Past and future have indeed become separated in our world. Even so, this separation does not suggest the end of history, but rather that we have reached a juncture at which the idea of history as accident reflects our situation of *extasis*. But to be in this situation means only that we are entangled in history: that it is no accident that we are where we are.

Where we are, more and more, is bored and fed-up. It would appear that *ennui*, which used to be called the "French malady," has been democratized in our time. Our word *boredom* is related to the French *bourrer*, to stuff or satiate. To be able to say "I'm fed up to here with you" or "I've taken as much as I can" amounts to the same thing: that I'm stuffed full, that there is more inside me than I want to have there, that there is no more interior space, no place left for me to take anything upon myself. How do you get someone else inside of you? How do you appropriate another? Complete boredom and total self-possession are one and the same. Self-fetishism is the prerequisite of boredom: "nothing 'out there' excites me, I am bored" can be said only by a person who has interiorized himself to such an extent that "he" is "inside"—that is, an idiot, a private person. If you were just me, if you were only my narcissistic projections, then I would be bored with you. Thus idiocy sees itself in others, is bored, and withdraws back further into its own *extasis*. Boredom is the luxury of the idiosyncratization of man.

Idiot man experiences the external world as undifferentiated accident, as an orderly, monotonous mechanism, as "out there." The world as abstract and withdrawn from the self: this is dissociation and *extasis*. Other people are not to be depended on. All that is reliable is abstract: the *law* and the idiotic self. Thus the problem of boredom is the problem of Hobbesian political theory: that others are not to be counted upon.

Idiot man has nothing to do. There are methods of order which function mechanically—like the free market of classical economics—which allocate value and meaning through the force of convention, without the need for human interference and activity, without organizational association among people. So long as you behave yourself you will have the privilege of boredom: this is the promise of our world. At least you will be out of debt to others: this is the logic of behavior. Where boredom is a widespread possibility, there also inner experience, being oneself alone, becomes the ground of authenticity. Being left alone by a mechanistic set of institutions which operate at a distance to take care of business (*laissez faire*) is the political psychology of boredom and the spectacle politics of cynicism and corruption; witness Watergate and investigations of the C.I.A.

Not to be able to do anything, not to have anything to do, not to know what to do: these are the statements of our boredom. Boredom is freedom from politics; freedom is the ability to be bored. This freedom-boredom is largely what we tried to export to South East Asia, though we called it the promise of democracy: don't tamper with the machine. Life is boring and monotonous where there is nothing different, where there is nothing in the world except what we put in it: this is the logic of both self-possession and imperialism.

The destruction of difference (as with Vietnam) proceeds on the analogy of cloning: to want to see only oneself over and over again, to take the other within the self, to make it (him, her) one's own. This process creates certain problems which characterize our time, strange-sounding problems and projects like "Vietnamization," or how to give the Vietnamese back to themselves. The sovereign or imperial self-consciousness is thus a prime subject for political theory.

Today, increasingly, it is this self which is "real" and "true," while the categories of reality and truthfulness decreasingly characterize our received beliefs, values, and institutions. Politics—generally understood as the activities of deception, manipulation, and domination in different kinds of war (on poverty, in Vietnam, of the sexes)—comes to be separate from people's experience. It is "something" done by others at a distance, by the government, by the unions, by the Viet Cong: it is somehow "unreal" and abstract, or as political scientists have been observing for a decade, "not salient" for most people.

To locate politics "out there" and to still care about it is a destructive and ultimately disillusioning thing. Many political activists of the sixties rejected "politics" of this sort, arguing that in being political, a person can get lost. To see that such politics involves a loss of self, of integrity, that such depersonalization was a synonym for the political, is a perception which leads to both this rejection of the political as "unreal" and to a conception of "new politics," wherein the "personal is political." Thus among the broad "middle class" sexual politics—women's liberation, and more recently men's liberation as well—is at home. Sexual politics is the politics "in here," in the private and hidden pains and terrors of interpersonal relations, in the bedroom and the workplace (which are always the same kind of place, the location of the creation and the recreation of life, as Marx put it).

Politics so viewed is something like afternoon television soap operas. It is a privileged politics, a privilege of class, a politics closely related to the experiences of boredom and cynicism with and about contemporary life. I say this about my politics as well. I have sometimes thought that the standard by which to evaluate the general quality of political life ought to be the full orgasmic gratification of its citizens, judging along with Wilhelm Reich that sexual repression is a political problem, particularly for the middle class. For the middle class, the body politic and (in N. O. Brown's phrase) *Love's Body* are related more clearly than for other classes. The middle class experiences enough leisure and powerlessness, enough boredom and cynicism, to enable its members to look at their personal lives and to "work" on the quality of their relationships with others. It is here that the project of becoming "real" has its roots.

The politics of "being oneself," what has been called the "politics of authenticity," is an often confessional politics which began with Rousseau. It has found its most recent theorist in Marshall Berman, who describes our society in this way:

Our society is filled with people who are ardently yearning and consciously striving for authenticity: moral philosophers who are exploring the idea of "self-realization"; psychiatrists who are working to develop and strengthen "ego-identity"; artists and writers . . . bent on creating works and living lives in which their deepest, truest selves will somehow be expressed; young people, hip or straight, seeking to "get themselves together," determined above all to "do their own thing"; countless anonymous men and women all over who are fighting, desperately and against all odds,

simply to preserve, to feel, to be themselves.
(*Authenticity*, p. 325)

Berman romanticizes his model of authenticity, *l'homme révolté* battling the "system," arguing that "one of the most important things for radical critics to point to is all the powerful feeling which the system tries to repress—in particular, everyman's sense of his own, unique, irreducible self." Berman calls this "radical liberalism" (*Authenticity*, pp. 324, 317). This heroic rejection of "society" says "No!" to them, to the system or establishment, by saying *"Laissez faire!"*—leave me alone, let me be. It is, and Berman understands this, a radicalism which is the fulfillment, not the rejection, of "the ideals" of modernity.

To be radical in this sense is to go to the root of modern Western political culture: the wisdom of authenticity and idiocy are one and the same, at the root.

In the next two chapters, we will trace this root from the beginnings of modern Western political theory through its culmination in the tradition of authenticity.

3
The Logic of Abstraction

> ... the "masterless men" of the sixteenth and
> seventeenth centuries ... were the heroes and
> villains of the age, cut loose from organic,
> hierarchical and particularist ties ... ambitious,
> calculating, irreverrent—insensitive to the ancient
> mysteries but not yet integrated into a modern
> social system. (Walzer, *Saints*, p. 23)

The Location of Politics and Freedom in Machiavelli and Luther

The beginnings of the history of modern Western political philosophy can be seen as a conversation between Machiavelli and Luther on the subject of "masterless men." In this conversation are embedded the central dilemmas and assumptions about the nature of human identity, expressed in D. H. Lawrence's words, "henceforth be masterless." The problem of the masterless man, cut off from traditional moorings, is the problem of discontinuity: the disruption of a common set of assumptions—a social epistemology—which ties together intent and action in meaningful, intersubjectively shared symbols.

Both Machiavelli and Luther knew that things were falling apart, that the principles of authority and belief which tie a people together were changing. Machiavelli asked questions like "How can a new prince seem old?," questioning in this formulation the basis of legitimacy and obedience, the meaning of citizenship and loyalty.

Machiavelli's answers to these questions have provided us with our dominant vocabulary of politics, a language of power and manipulation expressed in the commonsensical epithet *Machiavellian*. This language structures our understanding of the "external world" which is out there beyond our experience and which organizes our common perception of "the political."

Luther initiated the language and logic of an inner freedom which could endure within the individual in the face of even the most oppressive organizations of the "external world." Marx recognized the contribution of Luther as the true formulation of the problem of emancipation, correctly focused on the struggle of the layman "against his own inner priest, his priestly nature," as opposed to the conflict with any priest "external" to the individual. In locating freedom in the inwardness of man, Luther laid the ground for the modern idea of "authentic" man, free by the logic of privatization and interiorization of value. As Marx put it, Luther "freed man from outward religiosity by making religiosity the inwardness of man" (*Young Marx*, p. 258). Thus the "conversation" between Machiavelli and Luther is a dialogue between our dominant understandings of politics and freedom, the "outside" and the "inside" of us.

Machiavelli's concern was to point out to his masterless man, the prince, strategies for coping with the fact that given the breakdown of the integrated medieval Christian world-view, the time-honored Christian virtues were no longer dependable guidelines to action. Speaking of these virtues Machiavelli warned:

> . . . they cannot all be possessed or observed, human
> conditions not permitting of it . . . (*Prince*, p. 57)

The disjunction between that which is possessed in the inner recesses of a person (for example, intentions, faith, character) and what is manifest and observable in action (consequences or works) is expressed in the ambiguity of the word Machiavelli uses in the above passage, the past participle *osservado* ("observed"): it can be read either as denoting performance (as in "He observed the rules") or perception (as in "Some things cannot be observed"). This ambiguity contrasts with the use of the word *possessed*: while one might be said to possess all the Christian virtues (and Machiavelli clearly imagines that a man might be "good" in this sense, in an inner and intentional way), nonetheless these virtues can only be fully "observed" (performance) when they culminate in action which reflects this intentional sphere meaningfully (perception). That is, the meaning of one's action is relational in the sense in which it is *necessarily* for Machiavelli (as part of the nature of "human conditions") subject to interpretation by others.

But where things can be possessed which cannot be observed, where things are not as they appear, where one cannot, as Rousseau would later say, read the character of a man in his conduct, then the relationship between intent and action is problematic. The problem of the discontinuity between action and intention is also the absence of *stasis*, of a predictable and stable pattern of meaning, such as the "organic and hierarchical" ties of the medieval world-view. It is in this sense that Machiavelli understood his times as in *decline*, and saw decline as the absence of *stasis*. Thus the only guide to the man of worth (of *virtu*) was the judgment that his actions tended toward the reestablishment of *stasis*, of the condition of stability which Machiavelli expressed in *lo stato*.

The act of establishing (from *stabilis*, stable) a kingdom or a republic is valuable for Machiavelli because it constitutes the condition within which the relation between act and intent can be stabilized. The act of establishing (founding) cannot be judged (as one could judge a work of art) as a thing in itself. For Machiavelli, in contrast to "matters pertaining to the Arts, which shine by their intrinsic merits," things which "pertain to the actions and manners of men" are those "of which we do not possess such manifest evidence" (*Discourses*, p. 272). As Machiavelli says about Romulus, who slew his brother Remus but established Rome:

> . . . when the act accuses him, the result should excuse
> him; and when the result is good, as in the case of
> Romulus, it will always absolve him from blame.
> (*Discourses*, p. 139)

Thus any judgment about an act must bracket the "intrinsic merits" (or lack of such) as well as the subjective intention of the actor: action goes beyond intention. Though in a period of decline where act and intent are not tied together by dependable assumptions this statement necessarily entails ambiguity about the act and within the actor, Machiavelli argues that it is better "to act and to repent than not to act and to repent," with a view toward the possible establishment of common meaning, law, habits of stability, and political order.

But the undercurrent fear that what a man intends is altered and corrupted by the context in which his action appears and is "observed" leads as easily to an absolute focus not on the results of action but instead on the inner and unobservable subjectivity of the actor. Thus the problem of not knowing what a man truly is, of not being able to trust others (their praise or blame of one's actions being suspect, given the bifurcation of conduct and character), can lead to withdrawal from the contingency and uncertainty of a world without *stasis*. It is thus out of the experience of the ambiguities and anxieties of the lack of *stasis* that the Protestant Reformation, and Martin Luther especially, articulated the notion of an inner subjectivity, divorced from action and from the contingency of being observed by others: here Luther located what he called "Christian freedom."

Machiavelli's primary concern to return to a situation of *stasis* is paralleled by what is Luther's *ek-static* withdrawal from the world. While Machiavelli advises the masterless man to live outside himself, ever watchful of his reputation, always striving to be recognized in his action, Luther provides the masterless man with a way of responding to the problem of the discontinuity of intention and outcome, a way of coping with a situation in which

> . . . you do not know whether [a man] is a Christian or how long he will remain one, you cannot safely depend on him. (*Luther Selections*, p. 396)

Luther's solution, expressed in the phrase "I need nothing except faith" (p. 75), was to provide a formula for human relations which avoided the difficulties of contingency, so that men could conceptualize their worth without any consideration of "gratitude or ingratitude, of praise or blame, of gain or loss" (p. 76). Thus the locus of freedom and identity is shifted away from "external" societal mediation and is withdrawn into an inner realm in which the self can be "powerful in the midst of oppression," its power made perfect in weakness (pp. 63-64). This power is the beginnings of the modern concept of freedom as (in Sartre's words) the "withdrawal to found being." (See my note in Chapter 2 above, for a more contemporary and psychoanalytic expression of this conception [Binswanger] of power within powerlessness; also see the extended discussion of this idea in Chapter 5; for Sartre's conception, see pp. 116–17, near the end of Chapter 4.)

In the conversation between Machiavelli and Luther we have, then, two diametrically opposed responses to the absence of *stasis*: either live outside or within oneself. These responses are the germs from which the modern experience of *extasis* arises. This conversation will be continued by Hobbes and Rousseau: it is for Hobbes to provide the dominant metaphor for external *stasis* as living outside oneself, the metaphor of the marketplace; it is for Rousseau to provide the metaphor of "authentic" interiority (*ekstasis*) in the notion of being indebted to oneself alone. And it is in responding with Rousseau that the self, which faces its alternatives as *either* being-possessed by the logic of the marketplace *or* being its own inner possession, will experience itself as in *extasis*, where its alternatives, whether living within or without the self, are behavioral, that is, about possession.

In this sense it is Luther who begins the development of the psychology of the self which defines its identity and meaning as incapable of being taken from it: a self for which being is possessing. Such a self is related to that which is "not-self" through what I call the logic of abstraction. This logic is the gradual working out of the dichotomous alternatives of the possessive unconscious: possess or be-possessed. Of the three logical and historical stages of this development which I will next attempt to delineate—those of concretization, propriety, and primacy—Luther provides the logic of the first stage, the drawing together of an inner self in the attempt to escape the ambiguity and discontinuity of identity in the absence of *stasis*.

What follows, here, is an attempt to articulate the developmental stages, the genesis, of what I have called the "behavioral self." The "logic of abstraction" is essentially a heuristic model, applicable both to the history of modern Western political philosophy and to the psychology of the "behavioral" identity. Its utility lies in its ability to make intelligible some of the paradoxes and the despair of the history of modern Western political philosophy. The three stages of the model correspond to the philosophical dilemmas of Luther, Hobbes, and Rousseau respectively. (A more detailed analysis of the relationship between Hobbes and Rousseau is set forth in Chapters 4 and 5 of this book.)

The Concrete Self (The Self Posited)

The concrete self is characterized by the process of pulling itself together. In the absence of *stasis*, prior forms of meaning withdraw into abstraction, threatening the continuity of identity, the very "status" of connectedness with the world. Abstract external meaning elicits, in the thought of Martin Luther, an internal withdrawal, an "inner-migration" of meaning to compensate for the destruction of the significance of those visible and daily activities of work and sacrament which integrated the medieval world-view. The concrete self is a negation of this withdrawal of meaning, replacing contextual continuity with internal meaning, pulling together an identity which can be held onto. The self "aggregates itself" (becomes *concrete*, from *concretus*, aggregated), as subjectivity and inwardness in the face of being out-of-place in the world. As such, the concrete self is conditioned by a world of abstraction upon which it depends and to which it reacts. It grows together through withdrawal as it experiences "external" meaning withdrawing from it: I have therefore termed the concrete-self process the first stage in the logic of abstraction, the dialectical logic of withdrawal (*abstraction* from *abstractio*, withdrawal).

There is, however, in the withdrawal of the Lutheran concrete self, an incomplete resolution of the lack of *stasis*. The concrete self is tied by negative reference to an abstract Machiavellian externality. Its identity exists in a vacuum and is purely formal in the sense in which it is modeled after the experience of abstractness. All that this statement expresses is that the concrete self is the mirror image of the emptiness of the external world: it has no content, is simply inwardness. The concrete self is pure negativity but is bound, therefore, by that abstract externality which it negates. Having begun its withdrawal but realized it only formally, the self is incomplete until it reconceptualizes its relation to externality as a relationship to itself: that is, until it has a content of its own, until it incorporates externality as its own property. This incompleteness thus posits the second stage of the process of abstraction, that of propriety: the stage of the "proper" self.

The Proper Self (The Self Coming into Its Own)

The proper self (from *proprius*, one's own) is that self which relates to itself as form to content. While it is still related through negation to that which is not-self, its acquisition of a part of externality as its own property alters its relation to social or political reality. Reality becomes "realty" from the perspective of the proper self: that externality which is its own. Correspondingly the self acquires property in itself, develops a legal persona, personality, or content; in legal history we can trace the development of the idea of "personality" (personal movable goods) to the seventeenth century. During the historical period within which the proper self developed, the terms *personality* and *personalty* were interchangeable, and indicated the working out of the development of the self as its property. During this same period the terms *reality* and *realty* were synonymous as well and reflected the "connecting circumstances" among men, the perception of the external world from the viewpoint of the proper self. The development of private property does not in this sense *cause* personality to develop, but rather provides a metaphor through which the "concrete" self gives itself content. Prior to the widespread dominance of the metaphor of private property, the concrete self was overwhelmed by its abstract interiority and articulated that feeling as the God of the Lutheran Reformation.

Overwhelmed by its abstract inwardness, the concrete self without content could only assert its brute existence as given. In the face of the inestimable gifts of God (its own abstract inwardness) it speaks Luther's phrase: Here I stand.

If the concrete-self process corresponds to the development of the Protestant Reformation, then the development from the concrete- to the proper-self process covers roughly that period during which the self was seeking a content to parallel its inner form. It has reached its logical development when Locke declares that a man has property in himself. This period of development ends with the separation of the ideas of reality and realty, personality and personalty in the middle of the seventeenth century. The intervening period in which the words in each pair were synonymous reflects the growing period of the proper self.

In providing itself with content the proper self necessarily engages in antagonistic relations with others, understood as having as their own possibility a proprietary claim on themselves. Relations of propriety are antagonistic because the self as property is a scarce good. In any given situation the proper self must calculate its possessions: recognizing itself in others (what we call empathy) is that calculus which helps the proper self both to validate its fundamentally appropriate identity and to acknowledge that other proprietary claims exist. Mutual recognition is a manifestation not of respect but of tolerance. From the perspective of the proper self *all* relationships are simply to be tolerated, and then only to the extent to which they reinforce the possessive possibilities of any given situation. Encouraging propriety in others is a necessary consequence of the logic of the proper self: the self which is one's own must be validated, for it would not do to claim as property something which was not valued by others. The need for mutual recognition thus demands that while the proper self must be separate from others, must acknowledge property boundaries, it must also tolerate contractual relations with others against whom it can calculate its identity or position in any given situation. In its being-with-others it is both toward and against them: toward them to gain validation and against them to hold onto itself.

In the light of the need for mutual recognition of proper selves, interaction (the social-science term *co-behavior* is apt here) is role-playing, the wearing of a mask which protects the self behind it. In this way it is clear that the proper self is still abstract in that it is dependent upon externality in the form of validation or recognition by others, separate from and external but equivalent to the self.

This is Hobbes's dilemma. Hobbes recognized that dependence upon equals for the gift of recognition entailed despair where the desire for individual power (power after power unto death) was infinite. His solution was to attempt to transform this dependence into dependence on the "Sovereign." Such dependence was still, Rousseau thought, arbitrary. As Hegel understood, Rousseau attempted to transcend this arbitrariness in his conception of the general will.

Externality has become differentiated (one could say "personalized" here) by virtue of the content which the proper self acquires, but its dependence simply takes on relational dimensions: without the validation of others it has no security that its content is valuable. As such the proper self attempts two things simultaneously: (1) to fill itself up by more and more incorporation of the external world; (2) to demonstrate to others how much it holds and how well it holds itself.

How well it holds itself ("He holds himself well") depends upon the masks of character by which the proper self evaluates and compares itself with others. How much it holds is never enough: what is behind the mask is still dependent upon externality, still abstract. What Hobbes said about power is an accurate description of the proper self: it strives for power after power (possession after possession) until death. Externality retains its sway over that self which is only the illusion of an illusion, the mask which, if stripped away, reveals nothing. The mask itself is still a reminder of its lack of self-completion. Though the self relates itself to itself, the value of this internal relation is conditional upon recognition from others.

In Rousseau's dictum that the man is not the mask we find the first indication of the tension within the developmental stage of propriety, the tension which provides the dynamic toward the third possible identity for the self in the process of abstraction: the stage of self-possession in which the self no longer simply relates itself to itself as property but in doing so "participates" so completely with its world that externality ceases to exist, and with it, the need to tolerate relationship with or dependence on others.

The Primary Self (The Self Possessed)

The third stage in the development of the logic of abstraction consists of the attempt of the proper self to reconceptualize external reality by incorporating it into the self as a "sense" of reality. "Realty" is reality for the proper self, but despite appropriation of the external world, this formulation still entails relation with and dependence upon conditions outside of the self—especially in the need that one's property be recognized by others. The only alternative which can resolve this tension is one that totally collapses the external-internal distinction. This alternative is a form of what Piaget calls "primitive realism" and entails the assumption that the self is inseparable from its object-world. The proper self had sought efficacy through trying to hold onto the world as itself. But this was incomplete in that dependence upon an abstraction continued. Primitive realism, as complete egocentricity, denies the existence of an external world, completes the world within the self. Thus the self possessed, the prime, primitive, or "primary" self, is like a prime number in mathematics: it has no integral factors other than itself and one, is "related" only to "oneness," and this oneness is identical with itself. Relationship here becomes understandable in terms of what Lévy-Bruhl called the "participation mystique": the relationship between two phenomena which are regarded as identical, though there is no spatial or intelligible dependence or connection between them (*Primitive Mentality*). Piaget's description of children who, when asked how the clouds move, reply "Because I walk," is an example of the integration which the primary self achieves with respect to the internal-external dimension (*Child's Conception*, Ch. 7). As such it is applicable to that self-process which does not distinguish between autoplasticity and alloplasticity, between a change in the self and a change in environment. This is another way of talking about the self-process of "protean" man, and must be understood as an attempt to resolve the tensions of "propriety."

See my note in Chapter 2, page 58 above. The integration of self and environment which the prime self achieves is the logical development of the situation of *extasis*, and is definitive of the problem of "boredom." In the situation of being de-situated the integration of self and context can take place only *within* the self. The prime self is free from all personal dependence, and is most characteristic of the modality of boredom.

The notion of participation mystique entails the assumption of pure time without space: reality is essentially understood as an inner dimension which infinitely endures, and from which the "external" world is projected. This inner reality is neither contaminated by nor measured in terms of its externalizations. Here we have reached the completed picture of self-possession, the perfection of never finding anything outside the self but what the self has put there.

Thus the proper self disowns its relational existence, its personality—which it had acquired in order that its propriety be recognized and evaluated by others. The content which the self achieved, its identity as property, needed reinforcement from others: but that reinforcement (which I have called recognition) itself was a reminder of dependence. The proper self, which is able to contrast its content (its relation to itself) with its relational form (reinforcement), now separates content from form and deems its formal or relational identity (its personality) as inauthentic. It had "endured" relation so as to reinforce its content, so as to affirm an inner content which would endure. When it separates this inner content from its outer reinforcement it is left with pure duration.

Thus the mode of duration is the mode of the happening, of continuous and undifferentiated movement, of wholeness and inner integrity. The "purity" of duration is the escape from any interactional definition of the self-process; it is only because the self is whole, purely in touch with its own duration, that something happens in the world. From this point on the self acquires a "sixth sense": all of its relational possibilities will be understood as a "sense of." Thus reality is a "sense" of reality, efficacy is a "sense" of efficacy, and participation with its surroundings is understood, via the logic of the participation mystique, as a "sense" of participation. The completion of the logic of abstraction thus indicates the uniformly vicarious status of the experience of the primary self.

By completing the world within the self, the primary-self process achieves a position by virtue of which its behavior cannot be evaluated in terms of "external consequences." Meaning is no longer tied to a framework of interpretation: it has no limits. Consequently the realm of freedom for the primary self is infinite, but this freedom is infinitely inward in nature. Behavior is free only if it manifests the integrity of a world complete within the self: only if it expresses "the whole of the self." There are only inner criteria, such as wholeness and purity, which are applicable to the evaluation of an action, its freedom and significance.

Any spatial or contextual determinants of efficacy—the existence of limiting conditions on the potential for action—are nonexistent to the extent to which power, efficacy, and participation are identifiable only by their inner duration. Georges Sorel, building on Bergson, understood correctly that these assumptions are necessarily part of what he called "mythic" political activity. By removing all external limits on action, the participation mystique equates inner hopes with reality, and, in Sorel's words, this mythic form of consciousness "gives *complete reality* to the hopes of immediate action" (*Violence*, p. 45). The completeness of reality is, of course, completion of the world within the primary self; "the character of infinity" which Sorel attributes to myth is another way of saying that the final development of the logic of abstraction is to preclude the possibility of falsifying any claim of the primary self: its freedom cannot be evaluated by others for it is totally self-possessed.

In this third stage the self has changed itself qualitatively. By incorporating the dimension of action-in-the-world into itself, it has achieved a sense of self which it sought but could not find in relation to a world which it perceived as abstract. It had first to withdraw from that abstraction (the concrete self) and then take back a part of that abstraction as its own (the proper self). It passed into the third stage by taking the separation between self and world into the self, and then by denying that separation. In order to be able to view its desires as reality, to become inseparable from its objects, it was necessary for the self to destroy its dependence on a world which mediated desire and gratification, intention and action. Thus the primary self, in ceasing to accept definition through conditions outside itself, is in tension neither with itself nor with the world: it is decontextualized, in *extasis*.

The self which is complete unto itself brackets, in other words, a dimension of its experience. It is this bracketed dimension which Hegel referred to as the realm of human feelings and ideas, what he called "mere concepts," understood as "ephemeral existence, external contingency, opinion, unsubstantial appearance, falsity, illusion . . ." (*Right*, p. 14). Hegel suggested that a mode of etymological analysis might reveal precisely this nonessential dimension. It would be an "abstract and nonphilosophical method," which, he suggested, would deduce a definition

> from etymology or . . . by abstraction from particular
> cases, so that it is based on human feelings and ideas.
> The correctness of the definition is then made to lie in
> its correspondence with current ideas. This method
> neglects what is all-essential for science . . . the absolute
> necessity of the thing. (*Right*, p. 15)

This is the method which I have employed in the preceding discussion of the development of the modern self-process, one which emphasizes the conjunction of etymology with certain contemporary "human feelings and ideas" about loss, "propriety," and possession, treating the history of philosophy as indicative of particular fears and anxieties rooted in the contingencies of the application of the language and logic of private property to the experience of human identity.

Hegel was correct, I think, in asserting that this method does not discover necessity in historical process; rather, it provides a perspective in terms of which this process becomes intelligible in context rather than through any essential necessity. The necessity which Hegel discovered in historical process was the necessity of the will—the "activity of man in the widest sense"—which actualizes the principle, aim, or destiny of the idea of freedom and which as such is the "hidden, undeveloped essence" in history (*Philosophy of History*, p. 22). Yet when Hegel depicted the historical development of the will, what he isolated as its essential structure is, I suggest, the contingency of what we might call the "behavioral will": the will to possess. The structure of human activity in history is, for Hegel, manifested in the mode of possession. The will to possess is the fully developed logic of the primary self. In order to document the ways in which the hidden essence of history as Hegel understood it is intelligible in terms of the logic of the possessive unconscious, I will focus on Hegel's discussion of the development of personality in the *Philosophy of Right*, referring as well to his understanding of Luther, Hobbes, and Rousseau in the *Lectures on the History of Philosophy*, and to the conception of the human will which informs the *Philosophy of History*. My concern here is to demonstrate that Hegel's conception of historical necessity does indeed tap a hidden structure: the contingent, ideological structure of the assumptions of the possessive unconscious.

The Will to Possess

It is in the Protestant Reformation, in the emergence of the Lutheran faith, that, for Hegel, the beginnings of the highest expression of freedom lie. In Luther, he says,

> . . . the principle of subjectivity, of pure relation to me personally, i.e., freedom, is recognized, and not merely so, but it is demanded that in religious worship this alone should be considered. (*History of Philosophy*, Vol. 3, p. 149)

At the basis of the Reformation is

> . . . the *abstract* moment of a mind being within itself, of freedom, of coming to self; freedom signifies the life of the spirit in being turned back within itself in the particular content which appears as another; while spirit is not free if it allows this other-being . . . to exist in it as something foreign. In so far as spirit now goes on to knowledge, to spiritual determinations, and as it looks around and comes forth as a content, so far will it conduct itself therein as in its own domain, as in its concrete world, so to speak—and it will there really assert and possess its own. (*History of Philosophy*, Vol. 3, pp. 154-155; emphasis mine)

What Hegel terms "abstract" about Lutheran freedom is what I have called "concrete": that identity has turned inward, has *formally* aggregated itself as itself (Hegel says that it finds a "sense of being at home" with itself) (p. 149), but that it lacks a content for its formal freedom.

The search for this content is, for Hegel, the process by which personality is acquired. Hegel is not explicit about this process in his brief discussion of Hobbes in the *History of Philosophy*, but the meaning of personality as he develops it in the *Philosophy of Right* is precisely the Hobbesian position of the mutual recognition of proper selves. Hegel notes in the *History of Philosophy* that Hobbes's concern was to subject the particular will of the individual to a universal (the Laws of Nature) which is directed against the private will (*History of Philosophy*, Vol. 3, p. 318). We will see below the ways in which Hobbes formulates this problem. Here we may note that one metaphor which Hobbes utilizes to cope with the radically subjective and individualistic tendencies of his times is that of contract. When Hegel traces the development of the right of property into the sphere of contract he articulates the Hobbesian dilemma: how can radical subjectivity and dependence on others be reconciled?

While Lutheran freedom is purely subjective, the development of personality, Hegel argues, transcends this subjectivity:

> For personality . . . as inherently infinite and universal, the restriction of being only subjective is a contradiction and a nullity. Personality is that which struggles to lift itself above this restriction and to give itself reality, or in other words, to claim that external world as its own. (*Right*, p. 38)

A person, Hegel says, must "translate his freedom into an external sphere in order to exist as Idea" (*Right*, p. 40). In his property,

> . . . a person exists for the first time as reason. Even if my freedom is here realized first of all in an external thing, and so falsely realized, nevertheless abstract personality in its immediacy can have no other embodiment save one characterized by immediacy. (*Right*, pp. 235-236)

The immediate possession of external property is thus the first (still abstract and incomplete for Hegel) content of human freedom. Personality, the reality of the person, is here alienable: this is the case so long as the characteristics of personality are external. That externality is annulled only when personality is *idea*, not simply potential (*Right*, p. 53). It is in this sense that, for Hegel,

> It is my mind which of all things I can make most completely my own. (*Right*, p. 46)

That is, by becoming self-conscious of one's free will, by raising the idea of freedom to consciousness, personality becomes inalienable:

> It is only through [man's] self-conscious apprehension of [him]self as free, that he takes possession of himself and becomes his own property and no one else's. (*Right*, pp. 47-48)

In this the logic of the free will is appropriative:

> All things may become man's property, because man is free will and consequently is absolute, while what stands over against him lacks this quality. Thus everyone has the right to make his will the thing or to make the thing his will, or in other words to destroy the thing and transform it into his own. . . . Thus "to appropriate" means at bottom only to manifest the preeminence of my will over the thing and to prove that it is not absolute, is not an end in itself. (*Right*, addition to #44, p. 236)

[In the *Phenomenology of Mind*, Hegel discusses the logic of egoistic appropriation in his section on sense-certainty, and it is clear that there he presents this stage as *aufgehoben* through further dialectical stages of consciousness.]

In the introduction to the *Philosophy of History*, Hegel emphasizes the essential *mineness* of the will:

> That some conception of mine should be developed into act and existence, is my earnest desire: I wish to be satisfied by its execution. If I am to exert myself for any object, it must in some way or other be *my* object. In the accomplishment of such or such designs I must at the same time find *my* satisfaction. (p. 22; emphasis in original)

This characteristic mineness about an act of will is, Hegel says,

> . . . a consideration of especial importance *in our age*, when people are less than formerly influenced by reliance on others, and by authority; when, on the contrary, they devote their activities to a cause on the ground of their own understanding, their independent conviction and opinion. (p. 23; emphasis mine)

This passage, comparable to Tocqueville's judgment that dependence on concrete, existing others as a referent for identity was
increasingly absent in the nineteenth century, does not, for Hegel,
elicit concern for the loss of *traditional* authority or connectedness among men. Rather, it expresses the contingencies which
reinforce the essential quality of the movement of Spirit in history:

> Spirit . . . may be defined as that which has its center in
> itself. It has not a unity outside itself, but has already
> found it; it exists *in* and *with itself*. Matter has its
> essence out of itself; Spirit is *self-contained existence*
> (Bei-sich-selbst-seyn). Now this is Freedom, exactly. For
> if I am dependent, my being is referred to something
> else which I am not; I cannot exist independently of
> something external. I am free, on the contrary, when my
> existence depends upon myself. This self-contained
> existence of Spirit is none other than self-consciousness
> of one's own being. (*Philoscphy of History*, p. 17)

In the preceding passages the distinctions between necessity
and contingency and between Spirit and self are blurred. Hegel
acknowledges simultaneously the essential mineness of the will
and its particular importance given the contingencies of his times.
Similarly, his discussion of the necessary distinction between
Spirit and Matter concludes with reference to personal dependence. Compare the latter statement of the freedom of the self
with this passage from the introductory lecture on the *History of
Philosophy* where Hegel utilizes precisely the same logic in
speaking of absolute Spirit (Mind): only through withdrawal,
Hegel says,

> . . . does Mind attain its freedom, for that is free which is
> not connected with or dependent upon another. True
> self-possession and satisfaction are only to be found in
> this. (Vol. 1, p. 23)

In his inaugural address at the University of Heidelberg in 1816,
Hegel argued that during the Napoleonic period, Germany had
been preoccupied with the "petty interests of everyday life," the
deep concerns of "actuality" which had engrossed "all the powers
and forces of the mind." Thus occupied, Mind could not "look
within and withdraw into itself." But the problems of everyday

life had finally been solved by the emergence of the State, which had "swallowed up all other interests in its own." Thus Mind, which had "hitherto been prey to externalities," could "return within itself, come to itself again" (*History of Philosophy*, Vol. 1, p. xi).

Externality signifies being connected with others in the contingent concerns of everyday life. The organization of "externality" into the State removes everyday concerns of connectedness from the province of the self. To define connectedness as unfreedom (as Hegel does in the above passages with respect both to Spirit and to self) is to express the perspective of the possessive unconscious: that freedom is self-possession. The consolidation of the State is necessary for Hegel because the possessive subjectivity of the will cannot, even when it acquires property, be a sufficient guarantee of freedom. Property, Hegel argues, is an "existent" because it embodies the will, and therefore,

> ... from this point of view the "other" for which it exists can only be the will of another person. The relation of will to will is the true and proper ground in which freedom is existent. . . . The sphere of contract is made up of this mediation whereby I hold property not merely by means of a thing and my subjective will, but by means of another person's will as well and so hold it in virtue of my participation in a common will. (*Right*, p. 57)

Relationships between persons who own themselves and whose wills are essentially possessive must be contractual:

> Contract presupposes that the parties entering it recognize each other as persons and property owners. It is a relationship at the level of mind objective, and so contains and presupposes from the start the moment of recognition. (*Right*, Knox's comment, p. 57)

The moment of recognition is the moment in which reciprocal self-possession is acknowledged, which transforms the "private particularity of knowing and willing" into its "recognized actuality as the protection of property through the administration of justice" (*Right*, p. 134).

Marcuse's comment on Hegel speaks to this point:

> Hegel has removed the institution of private property
> from any contingent connection and has hypostatized it
> as an ontological relation. (*Reason and Revolution*,
> p. 193)

It is the introjection of the logic of external appropriation as a relationship of the self to itself which transforms contingency into ontology, raises the proper self to the status of the essence of the human will, and demands that recognition of one's selfhood originate in ownership.

Hegel saw the state's administration of justice as the embodiment of a universal (and common) will, and believed that Hobbes was correct that "the universal will is made to reside in the will of one monarch" (*History of Philosophy*, p. 318), or sovereign, and that this will could mediate private particularity by guaranteeing a right to property. Yet Hegel argued that Hobbes provided no way of distinguishing the "merely subjective will" of the sovereign from the rational, universal will which alone could provide such a guarantee.

Thus Hegel saw that Hobbes understood the dilemma of the proper self: that it needed validation by others in order to be truly free in its possessiveness. In arguing that Hobbes does not distinguish the subjective from the universal principle of sovereignty, Hegel implies that there is still arbitrariness and, as Rousseau would put it, personal dependence, embedded in Hobbes's conception. In fact, it is to Rousseau that Hegel turns in order to express the crucial distinction between subjective and universal sovereignty.

It was Rousseau, Hegel believed, in whom

> . . . the innermost principle of man, his unity with
> himself, is set forth as fundamental and brought to
> consciousness, so that man in himself acquired an
> infinite strength. (*History of Philosophy*, p. 401)

Hegel refers at some length to Rousseau's statement of the problem of the social contract, to protect person and property while ensuring that each individual, while associated, remains as free as before, and he notes (also on p. 401) that Rousseau's solution to this problem is that each is a member "by his own will." In this respect Hegel understood (I think correctly) that the central concern of Rousseau's political philosophy was freedom from personal (that is, arbitrary) dependence. Freedom from personal dependence makes it possible to unite subjective freedom with objective reason, or as Hegel says in his discussion of Rousseau:

> The universal will must really be the rational will, even if we are not conscious of the fact; the state is therefore not an association decreed by the arbitrary will of individuals. (*History of Philosophy*, p. 402)

The Rousseauan conception of the state is thus, for Hegel, the "first realization of freedom" (p. 402), and it is so because it is the guarantor which transforms the potential of personal freedom (personality) into actuality without personal dependence.

Thus, moving through the stages of Lutheran subjectivity (what I have called the concrete self), Hobbesian recognition (the proper self), and Rousseauan freedom from personal dependence (the primary self), Hegel depicts the progressive development of the logic of the behavioral will: the unfolding of a conception of the self and others, protected as well from dependence on one another as from their own possessive subjectivity.

The fully developed conception of the Rousseauan state was for Hegel a conception of reconciliation: "the objective and the subjective will are then reconciled, and present one identical homogeneous whole" (*Philosophy of History*, p. 39). This homogeneity is actual only where each particular subjectivity (individual) possesses property in himself (personality); but since each individual will is essentially possessive, one cannot guarantee one's personality by depending upon the will of another person. Thus there is the need, which Rousseau understood, to alienate each possessive subjectivity from itself, so that, as Rousseau put it, "each gives himself to all and to nobody." This paradox at the core of Rousseau is as well at the root of the fundamental tension between separation and unity in Hegel's work.

In his early theological writings Hegel explored the tension between intense subjectivity and what he called the union "free from all inner division," noting, significantly, that the human phenomenon of separation is manifested in the experience of possession:

> The one who sees the other in possession of a property must sense in the other the separate individuality which has willed this possession. (*Christianity*, p. 308)

It is love, Hegel argued, which strives to destroy separation, for it is ashamed of its own exclusiveness:

> Shame enters . . . through the presence of an [exclusive] personality or the sensing of an [exclusive] individuality. It is not a fear *for* what is mortal, for what is merely one's own, but rather a fear *of* it, a fear which vanishes as the separable element in the lover is diminished by his love. (p. 306)

For in love, "consciousness of a separate self disappears, and all distinction between the lovers is annulled" (p. 307). Yet Hegel concludes his fragment on love with the following passage:

> Since possession and property make up such an important part of man's life, cares and thoughts, even lovers cannot refrain from reflection on this aspect of their relations. Even if the use of the property is common to both, the right to its possession would remain undecided, and the thought of this right would never be forgotten, because everything which men possess has the legal form of property. But if the possessor gives the other the same right of possession as he himself, community of goods is still only the right of one or the other to the thing. (p. 308)

Possession is thus the essential limit on that which is common: to go beyond this limit is to go beyond, to sacrifice, the self. The tension between love and possession is the tension between community and personality, and derives from the ways in which personal or subjective experience have been understood in the modern West in terms of the logic of the possessive unconscious. Subjectivity presupposes, as Hegel saw, the ability of the self to establish a property relationship with itself, to claim, as Hegel said, its own dominion.

If one begins with the experience of a context in which personal identity is necessarily defined by the constraints of the language and logic of property, then interpersonal relationships will always raise the specter of subjection, of the loss of dominion and possessive control over oneself as property. Contractual relationships are the détente through which this tension is maintained, and in terms of which the despair of the behavioral self—torn between love and possession, loss and identity—is expressed. It is toward an understanding of this despair and especially of one dominant expression of it—the tradition of authenticity in modern Western political philosophy—that I now turn.

4
The Desperate Debtor and the Tradition of Authenticity

To have received from one, to whom we think ourselves equal, greater benefits than there is hope to requite, disposeth to counterfeit love; but really secret hatred; and puts a man into the estate of a desperate debtor, in that in declining the sight of his creditor, [he] tacitly wishes him there, where he might never see him more. (Thomas Hobbes, *Leviathan*, p. 81)

The Desperate Debtor

Buried beneath the mechanistic calculus, the geometric reasoning, and the metaphors of *homo economicus*, there lies, at the core of the writings of Thomas Hobbes, a landscape of despair, the realm of the desperate debtor. It is Hobbes who tells us, almost in passing, that gratitude is retribution and that the receiver seeks revenge. This is the despair of the behavioral self:

> For benefits oblige, and obligation is thraldom; and unrequitable obligation perpetual thraldom; which is to one's equal, hateful. But to have received benefits from one, whom we acknowledge for superior, inclines to love; because the obligation is no new depression; and cheerful acceptation, which men call gratitude, is such an honour done to the obliger, as is generally taken for retribution.
> Also to receive benefits, though from an equal, or inferior, as long as there is hope of requital, disposeth to love: for in the intention of the receiver, the obligation is of aid and service mutual; from whence proceedeth an emulation of who shall exceed in benefiting; the most

> noble and profitable contention possible; wherein the
> victor is pleased with his victory, and the other revenged
> by confessing it. (*Leviathan*, p. 81)

Hobbes, in certain respects like the early American Puritans, attempted to provide a framework to deal with the antinomian characteristics of seventeenth-century England. The problem which fascinated him was what he called the "madness" of his age, which had its roots in "private interpretation," either of the Scriptures ("everyman became a judge of religion, and an interpreter of the Scriptures to himself"—*Behemoth*, p. 28) or of public duty:

> ... the people in general were so ignorant of their duty,
> as that not one perhaps of ten thousand knew what right
> any man had to command him, or what necessity there
> was of King or Commonwealth, for which he was to part
> with his money against his will; but thought himself to
> be so much master of whatsoever he possessed, that it
> could not be taken from him upon any pretense of
> common safety without his consent. (*Behemoth*, p. 7)

Persons who were (as Hobbes put it) "possessed of an opinion of being inspired" (*Leviathan*, p. 63) were uncompromisingly mad, madness for Hobbes being a vehement desire for any one thing. Hobbes's political philosophy is located between the extremes of this madness on the one hand, and what he called "giddiness" on the other, giddiness being the desire for all things indifferently. Between madness and giddiness, between prideful claims and the cessation of desire, Hobbes, like Calvin before him and Freud after, structured a social psychology of indebtedness as an attack upon the deadly sin of prideful self-possession, which he saw as constitutive of the madness of his times.

This portion of the Western tradition, of which Hobbes, Calvin, and Freud are representative, assumes that indebtedness is the bond of human association, and that self-possession must be sacrificed for civil society to be possible. Prideful human aims and intentions, the desire for power after power until death, cannot be abolished from the nature of man, but they can be inhibited: Hobbes, Calvin, and Freud agree that the sin of pride is the central obstacle to human organization, never to be completely overcome, but rather to be mediated by mechanisms through which men can learn the logic of their indebtedness. On this assumption, civil society becomes a perpetual struggle for moderation, control, and order; civil life, a fragile artifice suspended between madness and giddiness.

The artifice of external civil life can be achieved only by teaching men that they are irredeemably indebted to and for "society," and that this indebtedness should be accepted with gratitude. The individual who is in this way indebted is neither giddy nor mad: he is dependent for his sense of worth upon an artificial unity (society) which is "outside" of him; his desires are neither undisciplined nor self-aggrandizing, but are organized by a power which stands above him, in the face of which he stands in awe.

"Rage" was, for Hobbes, the expression of madness in action; being based on excessive opinion of one's self combined with envy of others, rage culminated in the destruction of the fragile social artifact, revealing the chaos which underlay social control. The "madness of the multitude" was manifest for Hobbes in those who "clamour, strike and throw stones" against those by whom they had been previously "protected and secured from injury" (*Leviathan*, p. 63).

What Hobbes called "rage," Freud termed "the primary mutual hostility of human beings," from which civilization was perpetually threatened with disintegration. Thus "aim-inhibited relationships" were necessary for civil life to be possible, and the characteristic societal commandment against the sin of pride—love thy neighbor as thyself—was a method for setting limits on aggressive instincts; and it was justified, as Freud said, because "nothing else runs so strongly counter to the original nature of man (*Civilization*, p. 59). John Calvin put it this way:

> Since men were born in such a state that they are all too
> much inclined to self-love—and, however much they
> deviate from truth, they still keep self-love—there was
> no need of a law which would increase or rather
> enkindle this already excessive love. (*Institutes*, p. 417)

The principle of what Calvin called "rightly directed love" (aim inhibition) teaches the poverty of human nature, the destructiveness of human aims and intentions. Desire must be deflected from its objects, so that products can be produced which go so far beyond the intentions of their producers that their production becomes abstract and anonymous. Thus the gifts of God—civil society, civilization, the products that no one produces, but for which all are indebted—come to symbolize a power which, to borrow from Kierkegaard, is a nothing which is everything. *Sui generis*, ever present, abstract and artificial, this power demands gratitude in order to reinforce the political psychology of indebtedness.

Gratitude was, for Hobbes, the fourth law of nature, without which the bonds of civil indebtedness could not function. Hobbes maintained that giving was a form of enslaving, that "benefits oblige, and obligation is thraldom." Great gifts especially, gifts which could never be repaid, generate intense hatred when given by one's equal, placing men into the "estate of a desperate debtor." So Hobbes argued, and here he expresses the etymological sense of the word *obligation*, from the Latin *ligare*, to tie or to bind, found in the medieval relation of "liegeman" (*liege*, from *ligare*, via *ligius*), "bound" to his lord, as property. But the despair of the debtor is rooted not in being bound but in being indebted to one's equals for one's sense of worth or identity. Since some principle of equality was necessary to Hobbes's critique of pride, but since the madness of his times—the rage against former "protectors" which expressed the growing condition which Hegel described as "masters without slaves and slaves without masters"—was destroying the concrete bonds of the liegeman, how, Hobbes asks, can the desperation of the debtor be avoided?

Hobbes, then, tried to separate despair and indebtedness. He thought that if men could learn to receive the benefits of civilization (the gift which could never be repaid) from one "whom we acknowledge for superior," gratitude would be possible, and acceptance would replace despair. Indebtedness must be accepted, in other words, on principle, must be abstract and impersonal, must express dependence upon the fundamental principle of civilization itself: this principle Hobbes called "the Sovereign." Thus members of the body politic could avoid concrete indebtedness or dependence "one of another" (which generated hatred) so long as "they depend only on the sovereign" (*Leviathan*, p. 418).

Abstract indebtedness, dependence upon a principle or power identified with the perpetuation of civilization itself, based upon aim inhibition, transforms prideful self-possession in a dual experience of anonymity: individuals simultaneously are anonymous one to another (they "cohere together" as Hobbes says), and are bound by obligation to an anonymous and generalized principle which guarantees their coherence.

Hobbes's remarkable innovation was to preserve equality of indebtedness through recourse to the principle of abstract dependence upon the Sovereign while simultaneously introducing the market metaphor as a guarantee that with respect to one another, people could make no claims to absolute worth. Thus his statement about personal identity, that a man's worth is his price and therefore a thing dependent on others, is directed against the *madness* of self-possession: no man can calculate his *own* worth; the market and the Sovereign preserve "coherence," and men are free from personal dependence on concrete others, free from the "despair" of indebtedness, though not from indebtedness itself.

Thus Hobbes presents a conception of an abstract and generalized principle of dependence, an "otherness" which separates prideful intention and action by enforcing an anonymous coherence among men. And this anonymity, the denial of absolute worth to the individual, is still problematic in Hobbes's attempts to alleviate the condition of the desperate debtor. For there is still an "externality" to indebtedness regardless of how abstract that indebtedness is understood to be, still a dependence over which the behavioral self despairs. Hence it is, as we have seen, for Rousseau to take the Hobbesian principles and internalize them: to argue that the only experience of indebtedness which abolishes behavioral despair is indebtedness to oneself alone. In this argument Rousseau returns to the Lutheran position, to the notion of power within powerlessness, now understood as an internal relation of ownership of the self to itself. These outlooks are the beginnings of the modern tradition of "authenticity," anticipated by Luther, its beginnings rooted in the interiorization of freedom, but incomplete until it finally discovers, through Hobbes, the possibilities of viewing the self as property.

The search for power within powerlessness which is characteristic of the tradition of authenticity is an attempt to reclaim as one's own that action which, in the name of aim inhibition, has been defined as beyond intention. The concern for authenticity expresses a struggle between the potentially authentic actor and a generalized, abstract power which mediates intention and action. The character of this power is its anonymity: it threatens the self with a loss of control over its acts and responsibility for them. This power, variously termed "society" (J. S. Mill), "public esteem" (Rousseau), "the public" (Kierkegaard), the "they" (Heidegger), or most directly the "other" (Sartre), threatens the freedom of the self: its negation is the search for an authentic self which the actor can hold onto.

Many of the problems which characterize the tradition of modern Western political philosophy—the relationship between self and society and the tension between power and freedom particularly—are logical extensions of the dilemmas of the desperate debtor.

These timeless "problems," which from the contemporary positivist perspective are dismissed as "metaphysical," are, I would argue, meaningful within the context of this despair. Their "timelessness" expresses neither something essential nor something senseless (or as the positivists would say, "unverifiable"). Rather, these problems are intelligible in that they reflect the conundrum of a tradition which has continuity in the degree to which it does not see through its characteristic assumptions. Continuity which entails the adoption of self-perpetuating dilemmas is not, it seems to me, to be valued for itself. The "problem" of what Sartre calls "the reef of solipsism" is a good example: solipsism is the philosophical expression of powerlessness, the gap which exists between the self and the other where certain specific assumptions about the nature of human action are perceived as inevitable. Solipsism is more instructive as a symptom; thus we might better ask: what assumptions must hold for solipsism to be problematic?

In Plato's *Symposium*, the physician Eryximachus argues that the art of the medical practitioner is to "reconcile the jarring elements of the body, and to force them, as it were, to fall in love with one another" (*Dialogues*, p. 186d). What I am suggesting is that much of modern Western political philosophy has been the reconciling of contradictory assumptions about the nature of the body politic, holding on to paradox and "timeless" problems as a compensation for not being able to break through the spurious dichotomies which emanate from the assumptions of the logic of behavior. Dichotomous thinking is an exercise in futility, and the pursuit of the logic of possession leads, as we will see in Sartre, to the definition of man as a "futile passion." Strung out on the forced love of jarring opposites, Sartrean man draws to its logical conclusion the systematically compensatory quality of modern political philosophy, its "timeless futility."

That our freedom is such that our passions are infinite and futile entails certain quite specific assumptions about the nature of need and desire. These assumptions are structured by the logic of behavior. In the following discussion of the tradition of authenticity I will utilize this logic in order to make intelligible a series of dichotomies, futilities, and paradoxes which constitute the madness of one dominant way of thinking about politics in the modern world. The focus is on what I refer to as the "tradition of authentic self-possession," and the sections which follow attempt both to define this tradition and to suggest the ways in which its assumptions illuminate present problems in political philosophy.

Part of my concern here is to explore the persistent series of dichotomies which this tradition presents, as a problem in itself: the problem of our tendency to paradoxical resolution of dichotomous assumptions. The assumption that serious thought about politics entails this recourse to paradox depends upon a prior claim to the effect that the only alternative to paradox is to embrace one extreme of some fundamental either/or. Rousseau is quite explicit about this:

> Common readers, pardon my paradoxes: they must be made when one thinks seriously; and, whatever you may say, I would rather be a man of paradoxes than a man of prejudices. (*Discourses*, p. 25)

This very fundamental either/or, either paradox or prejudice, is at the basis of much contemporary professional writing on the history of political philosophy. To accept it demands that our study should ferret out either the subtle and perhaps tragic paradoxes of the human condition or else the absurdity and unverifiability of metaphysical, ideological, or "prejudicial" assertions. In my view, neither the fascination with paradox nor the attempt to reduce complexity to nonsense or prejudice is very productive. My attempt here is for some middle ground of intelligibility: where paradox is understandable as a defense against recognizing the despair of the behavioral self, whose only alternatives are about possession. The paradoxical characteristics of the tradition of authentic self-possession are an outgrowth of the assumption that people are related by virtue of their separation. An examination of the extension of this assumption into a theory which defines authentic freedom as self-possession is the substantive concern of the following.

Rousseau: Freedom as the Cessation of Need

> "Indeed, what yoke could be imposed on men who need nothing?" (*Discourses*, p. 36)

Rousseau first described the gap, the separation, between being oneself and being a member of the state. He knew that in the modern West, to be both a man and a citizen would be a miracle. Recognizing that being yourself and being a citizen had come to be two different things, Rousseau turned his attention to both concerns separately. He wrote the *Social Contract* to show what it would mean to be a citizen, given man as he is. This vision of a state in which people must be "forced to be free" raises the specter of all totalitarian manifestations in the name of greater genuine collective identity and totalistic community.

Rousseau wrote *Emile* to show, on the other side of the separation, what it would mean to be a man given that one could not be a citizen, but only at best a barbarian in Paris. In *Emile* the psychology of being a man is presented as learning to live within oneself. In this difference, Rousseau's vision anticipates the tradition of authenticity in its development of the logic of separation from others as the basis of personal strength and virtue. It is this anticipation which I will explore here.

The quality which defined modernity as Rousseau understood it was the separation of the experiences of being and seeming. Modern political philosophy since Machiavelli had explored the discontinuity between being and seeming which arose when an actor, because he was seen and interpreted by others, might appear as something he was not, since he was judged by the consequences of his actions, not by some essential character which was evident in his "intent." For Rousseau, this problem becomes expressed as the lack of transparency of human intentions, the lack of congruence between what he calls conduct and character. Rousseau argues that the most characteristic art of modernity is the art of pleasing others, and he suggests that once this art is practiced then no longer is that situation present where "differences of conduct announced at first glance those of character" (*Discourses*, p. 37). How it came to be necessary "to appear to be other than what one in fact was" (*Discourses*, pp. 1-55) is the question which led Rousseau to explore the nature of human need.

In answering this question Rousseau begins from the position that all of the effort of modern man is directed toward two objects: achieving the commodities of life for oneself and seeking consideration from others (*Discourses*, p. 223). With respect to both objects, the problem which Rousseau isolates is that of being dependent for one's pleasure upon a condition outside the self. With respect to both material and considerational needs, this dependence is problematic in that it offers, Rousseau argues, only pleasure without happiness. Pleasure without happiness occurs when false and superfluous desires are perceived as true needs. To attempt to gratify such a "need" is to be enslaved into wanting more. Thus the acquisition of commodities "through habit . . . degenerated into true needs," and deprivation of commodities became, for modern man, "more cruel than possessing them was sweet": people were "unhappy to lose them without being happy to possess them" (*Discourses*, p. 147).

This problem of depending upon the externality of material possessions for one's happiness is exacerbated when the object of dependence is not simply a commodity, when that object is the consideration of others. In seeking this object there is more than the hollow search after that which can never be achieved (security in external property), for in addition there is the loss of the ability to see and to know oneself. To come to see ourselves as others see us, through their eyes, is to acquire a set of desires which, Rousseau says, "can only be satisfied with the help of others" (*Emile*, p. 48). These desires "which are not true needs" subject the self to external manipulation, so that "as soon as you are obliged to see with another's eyes you must will what he wills" (*Emile*, p. 48)

This perspective, the self viewed as a reflection of others, means that a man who is "always outside of himself, knows how to live only in the opinion of others; and it is from their judgment alone that he draws the sentiment of his own existence" (*Discourses*, p. 179). Seeing oneself in the reflection of society's mirror means that "everything is reduced to appearances . . . becomes factitious and deceptive." In the degree to which this reflection is definitive of one's identity, "always asking others what we are and never daring to question ourselves on this subject," men acquire a "deceitful and frivolous exterior . . . and pleasure without happiness" (*Discourses*, p. 180).

It is then, for Rousseau, the phenomenon of possession which is a consistent problem in the interior of both material and considerational dependence. Needing the help of others, being able to compare oneself with others, being injured by others—all are understood on the basis of the development of the "idea" of property among men: problems of dependence are problems of possession. In his quotation of the Lockean dictum that "where there is no property there is no injustice," Rousseau substitutes "injury" for "injustice," in order to make his point: that it is need of others and therefore the possibility of being injured by them which is the problematic social psychology of indebtedness (*Discourses*, p.

150). Thus: ". . . from the moment one man needed the help of another . . . equality disappeared, property was introduced, labor became necessary . . ." (*Discourses*, p. 151). When Rousseau asks, ". . . what can be the chains of dependence among men who possess nothing?" he means, therefore, what would it be like to imagine a world in which people did not need one another, and in which no value was placed on "public esteem"?

This world, prior to comparative evaluation, sentiments of preference and jealousy, where there is neither past nor future, neither consideration nor contempt, Rousseau calls *the state of nature*. It is out of this condition that man fell when "each one began to look at the others and to want to be looked at himself, and public esteem had a value" (*Discourses*, p. 149). It is the look of others which is the symbol of man's enslavement.

Societal need is bound up with artificial moral dependencies ("the moral element of love is an artificial sentiment born of the usage of society—*Discourses*, p. 135). In contrast, Rousseau's vision of the natural state is a picture of the integration of conduct and character where man is "subject to few passions and self-sufficient," with "no need of his fellow man" (*Discourses*, p. 137). Since men are at-a-loss when deprived of the presence of others, imagine, in contrast, what it would be like not to have such need: no deficiency would be possible, therefore no deprivation. To translate his passage on commodity dependence into the problem of depending on others: being deprived of others is more cruel than possessing them is sweet, because to need others is to be possessed by them; so in order to avoid possession, cease to need.

Rousseau clearly understood that this ceasing was an impossibility. And yet the whole of Rousseau's teaching is informed by this concern. Whether he is speaking of the qualities which make nations free or the character of the citizen noble, he speaks of the avoidance of particular dependence. What he says about that people which is a fit subject for legislation—that it must be one "which can do without other peoples, and without which all others can do" (*Social Contract*, p. 49)—is the prerequisite as well for the general educational theory which he develops in *Emile*. The paradox which is associated with Rousseau's conception of the law, that the individual who refuses to obey the general will must be "forced to be free," is rooted in this idea that freedom is the avoidance of personal dependence on others. What Rousseau called the "key to the workings of the political machine" is that in forcing man to be free, in giving each citizen to his country, obedience to the law "secures him against all personal dependence" (*Social Contract*, p. 18). This security makes it possible to imagine the logic of nature at work in the law, so that "each man, in giving himself to all, gives himself to nobody" (p. 14).

Rousseau is quite consistent in arguing that an authentic education for modern man (one "by nature") must teach the avoidance of interpersonal dependence. In this connection, Rousseau discusses in *Emile* two forms of dependence: dependence on things and dependence on men. Dependence on things is the work of nature, is "non-moral, does no injury to liberty and begets no vices"; dependence on men is the work of society, "gives rise to every kind of vice, and through this master and slave become mutually depraved" (p. 49).

In his assumptions about both public and private education, Rousseau distinguishes always the strength of nature (independence, self-sufficiency) from the weakness of society (dependence on public opinion, on other men). The weakness of society is hidden beneath what appears to be a form of power, which for Rousseau, because it entails the experience of contingency, is no power at all. Power must be total if it is to be real, and only as a scarce good, to be possessed in the avoidance of personal dependence, can it be secured for the individual:

> Your freedom and your power extend as far and no
> further than your natural strength; anything more is but
> slavery, deceit and trickery. Power itself is service when
> it depends on public opinion; for you are dependent on
> the prejudices of others when you rule them by means of
> those prejudices. To lead them as you will, they must be
> led as they will. They have only to change their way of
> thinking and you are forced to change your course of
> action. (*Emile*, p. 47)

To be forced to change your way of action when others change their way of evaluating your acts, to take others into consideration as a part of the field in which you act, is the essence of contingency. To avoid this experience is, for Rousseau, the substance of freedom: give yourself to nobody, "live your own life and you will no longer be wretched" (p. 47). Relationship demands indebtedness, involves a debtor and creditor, a giver and a receiver; this duality is inevitable. One must learn, then, how to avoid the perils of contingency and relationship; it is this lesson which Emile acquires early in his education:

He thinks not of others but of himself, and prefers that
others do the same. He makes no claims upon them, and
acknowledges no debt to them. He is alone in the midst
of human society, he depends upon himself alone.
(*Emile*, p. 170)

Authentic education is learning the wisdom of Robinson
Crusoe, learning to live in the social world *as if* it were Crusoe's
island, as if one were "deprived of the help of his fellow men."
Crusoe's condition, Rousseau notes, is not Emile's own; but he
should use it as the standard of comparison for all other conditions, a standard applicable to the perspective of a "solitary man"
(*Emile*, p. 147). From this perspective the strength of natural man,
"always carrying oneself, so to speak, entirely with one" (*Discourses*, p. 107), can be preserved amidst the corruptions of society. Thus Emile carries Crusoe's island around with him as if it
were his own condition, as if he were a solitary individual, deprived of the help of his fellow men. The acting out of these as-if
assumptions functions to depersonalize one's connections with
others to the point at which the "as if" becomes redundant. There
can be no indebtedness because there are no others, no definitive,
connecting relationships with others, no contingency for the self
which carries itself "entirely with" itself.

Yet Rousseau is aware that the "as if" is the best that men can
do. Relatedness and need are inevitable human "weaknesses,"
dependency is unavoidable. A paradoxical interpretation of Rousseau would emphasize that in the end, pleasure without happiness
is part of the human lot, men being, after all, not gods:

Man's weakness makes him sociable. . . . Every affection
is a sign of insufficiency; if each of us had no need of
others, we should hardly think of associating with them.
So our frail happiness has its roots in our weakness. A
really happy man is a hermit. God only enjoys absolute
happiness; but which of us has any idea what that
means? If any imperfect creature were self-sufficing,
what would he have to enjoy? . . . I do not understand
how one who has need of nothing could love anything,
nor . . . how he who loves nothing can be happy. (*Emile*,
p. 182)

God is absolutely happy because he does not need men. Human
need is an insufficiency, a lack. Goodness, for Rousseau, compen-

sates for this insufficiency by narrowing the limits within which contingency and insufficiency can be experienced:

> So it is the fewness of his needs, the narrow limits
> within which he can compare himself with others, that
> makes a man really good; what makes him really bad is a
> multiplicity of needs and dependence on the opinions of
> others. . . . True, man cannot always live alone, and it
> will be hard therefore to remain good . . . the dangers of
> social life demand that the necessary skill and care shall
> be devoted to guarding the human heart against the
> depravity which springs from fresh needs. (*Emile*,
> p. 175)

Man in modern society *is* this depravity, this insufficiency of being himself. As such, human being is indebtedness: ". . . since every man owes all that he is, he can only pay his own debt" (*Emile*, p. 158). Here it would appear that Rousseau acknowledges the basic sociality of human identity. But if a man owes all that he is, if he is indebtedness, what does he have of his own to repay with? From within the logic of the possessive unconscious, the logic of indebtedness is infinite: any form of genuine connectedness to others, to one's past or future, adds another debt which cannot be repaid. Indifference to the continual threat of contingency and dependence, what Nietzsche called "forgetfulness," is therefore necessary if one is to preserve an ordered control over one's debts: one must learn how not to "acknowledge" them. It is this structured indifference which is central to Rousseau's vision of the state of nature, by the logic of which the individual

> . . . can have neither foresight nor curiosity. The
> spectacle of nature becomes indifferent to him by dint
> of becoming familiar. There is always the same order,
> there are always the same revolutions. . . . His soul,
> agitated by nothing, is given over to the sole sentiment
> of its present existence without any idea of the future.
> (*Discourses*, p. 117)

This vision of the state of nature is precisely the vision which Carlos Castaneda has popularized through his characterization of Don Juan. It is this perspective which is agitated by nothing that is the core of Castaneda's conception of the warrior, and of his ethic of "controlled folly" which Don Juan expresses in these words: "I am happy that you finally asked me about my controlled folly after so many years, and yet it wouldn't have mattered to me in the least if you had never asked. Yet I have chosen to feel happy, as if I care, that you asked, as if it would matter that I care. That is controlled folly" (*Reality*, p. 99). That is what Nietzsche called "cynical innocence," the best and the worst of idiocy.

Situated between past and future, man by nature is so absorbed in the present that the qualifying dimensions of temporality, change, and contingency do not matter: he is agitated by nothing, indebted to himself alone.

Only by disengaging himself from the mirage of social judgment can man repay his debt. The mask, Rousseau argues, is not the man:

> The man of the world almost always wears a mask. He is scarcely ever himself and is almost a stranger to himself; he is ill at ease when he is forced into his own company. Not what he is, but what he seems, is all he cares for. (*Emile*, p. 191)

The mask is societal identity, a performance which is contingent on the judgment of others, a reflection, an appearance beneath which a man is himself. The state which Rousseau uses to contrast with the state of nature is the *state of reflection* (*reflexion*), and he means this word in a double sense. Reflection is both a mode of thought by which one calculates his connections, draws up his accounts of social indebtedness, and the process by which these debts are acquired. It is thus both in the recesses of human consciousness as "excesses of all kinds, immoderate ecstasies of all the passions, . . . numerous sorrows and afflictions . . . by which souls are perpetually tormented" (*Discourses*, p. 110), and is well-rooted in the social practice of learning to please others, seeing oneself "reflected" back to oneself through the mirror of "public esteem."

The "reflective" mode of consciousness is thus a form of *extasis*, in which one is carried away by his passions (ecstasy), or is carried out of himself by dependence on the judgment of others. Where a man's worth is his price, a thing "dependent on the need and judgment of another" (Hobbes), all that a man knows of himself is his reflection. The coming of the state of reflection means that people become "weak, fearful and servile" (*Discourses*, p. 111). This servility is the logical outgrowth of indebtedness, of an identity which is dependent on external demand. Hobbes, again, expresses so succinctly what Rousseau rejects:

> . . . as in other things, so in men, not the seller, but the
> buyer determines the price. For let a man, as most men
> do, rate themselves at the highest value they can; yet
> their true value is no more than it is esteemed by others.
> (*Leviathan*, p. 73)

As Rousseau put it:

> . . . since the bonds of servitude are formed only from
> the mutual dependence of men and the reciprocal needs
> that unite them, it is impossible to enslave a man
> without first putting him in the position of being unable
> to do without another. (*Discourses*, p. 140)

For Rousseau, the problem of reflection both begins and is
overcome through the idea of property. The first person who took
a plot of land and said "this is mine" was the true founder of civil
society (*Discourses*, p. 141). To be able to say about one's own
identity, "this is mine and no other's," is to attempt to transcend
the societal state of reflection by internalizing the logic of indebtedness. Man, by nature, lives "within himself" (p. 179). In order
to get in touch with this nature, Rousseauan man must separate
himself from others so as to cease to be a stranger to himself. His
desires, in other words, must be limited to those which he himself
can fulfill; those "reciprocal needs" which can only be satisfied
with the help of others are the source of human enslavement. To
live within oneself is the beginning of freedom.

The locus of identity for Rousseau is Crusoe's island; in the
writings of Kierkegaard, the aesthetic metaphor for the modern
self is a feudal castle. Both metaphors express the same idea: the
self as one's own, one's authentic property. I want to turn here to
the Kierkegaardian contribution to the tradition of authentic self-
possession.

The Kierkegaardian Legacy

> Carking care is my feudal castle. It is built like an
> eagle's nest upon the peak of a mountain lost in the
> clouds. No one can take it by storm. From this abode I
> dart down into the world of reality to seize my prey; but
> I do not remain down there, I bear my quarry aloft to my
> stronghold. My booty is a picture I weave into the

tapestries of my palace. There I live as one dead. I
immerse everything I have experienced in a baptism of
forgetfulness unto an eternal remembrance. Everything
temporal and contingent is forgotten and erased.
(Kierkegaard, *Either/Or*, Vol. 1, p. 41—the "aesthetic"
perspective)

In 1848, in the midst of political conflict throughout Europe,
Søren Kierkegaard documented a different sort of strife: the despair in the struggle to be oneself. What he said then could hardly
be said today: "... a self is the thing the world is least apt to
inquire about." What he understood to be the greatest human
danger, "losing one's own self" (*Sickness*, p. 165), and the most
important human project, "to will to be that self which one truly
is" (p. 153), have become the danger and search of an age. As with
other untimely men, Kierkegaard's time has come: ours is an age
of self-fetishism, where identity, autonomy, selfhood, and authenticity are words to conjure with, where self-actualization and
humanism have become synonyms to many.

Kierkegaard maintained that the "situation" of despair (*Sickness*, p. 153) was the result of what he called that "relation which
relates itself to itself":

... the relation to himself a man cannot get rid of, any
more than he can get rid of himself, which moreover is
one and the same thing, since the self is the relationship
to oneself. (*Sickness*, p. 150)

For Kierkegaard, this relation which relates itself to itself (the
self) is constituted by "another" (God), so that in relating itself to
itself the self simultaneously relates itself to another, to "the
power which posited it" (*Sickness*, p. 147). Thus the self-relation
is as well essentially a relationship to the "absolute other." (For a
discussion of the idea of the absolute other in Kierkegaard, see
Wahl, *Existentialism*, p. 6.) Kierkegaard emphasized the particularity of this relationship to the absolute (the standpoint of faith),
in the sense that its character was determined apart from all forms
of contingent societal mediation. [Compare D. Swenson's discussion of this aspect of Kierkegaard's work (quoted in Lowrie's introduction to *Fear*, p. 15) in which he argues that every form of
what he calls a "universal intermediary" (including "community,
state, humanity, tradition") is dispensed with from the perspective
of faith.] That is, the self must find itself while avoiding being

taken in by, or as Kierkegaard says "defrauded," by "the others":

> ... while one sort of despair plunges wildly into the
> infinite and loses itself, a second sort permits itself as it
> were to be defrauded by "the others." By seeing the
> multitude of men about it, by getting engaged in all sorts
> of worldly affairs, by becoming wise about how things go
> in this world, such a man forgets himself, forgets what
> his name is (in the divine understanding of it), does not
> dare to believe in himself, finds it too venturesome a
> thing to be himself, far easier and safer to be like the
> others, to become an imitation, a number, a cipher in the
> crowd. (*Sickness*, pp. 166-167)

In Kierkegaard's ethical writings, this same logic, namely that
there is a distinction between getting lost in the midst of a contingent and external world and finding the self, emerges as a distinction between "external" and "internal" history. What from the religious point of view involves the difference between "the others"
and the "absolute other," from the ethical point of view involves
the distinction between conquering and possessing:

> The conquering nature is constantly outside himself, the
> possessive nature within himself; hence, the former has
> external history, the latter has internal history.
> (*Either/Or*, Vol. 2, p. 137)

From both the religious and ethical perspectives Kierkegaard is at
pains to point out that one might win the world and lose his soul,
that one might achieve reputation in the eyes of others, might
conquer obstacles in the "external" world in so doing, but that so
long as one "does not possess himself, he is not himself" (*Sickness*, p. 152).

In both the ethical and religious writings of Kierkegaard, though
the self is understood to be relational, the essence of relation is
the absence of contingent mediation by other individuals. The self
relates to itself *and* to the absolute in the religious sense precisely
because it has extricated itself from definitive relations with concrete others.

Kierkegaard's social criticism begins with the perception that for
the modern age, relationship has become reduced to what he calls
a "colourless cohesion" (*Present Age*, pp. 43-44), and that the individual is "conscious of belonging in all things to an abstraction

to which he is subjected by reflection" (p. 53). This presupposes the Hobbesian conception of externality: men do not depend upon one another, they cohere together, dependent only on the abstract artifact of sovereignty. But where Hobbes had argued that the only conceivably stable principle of unification in such a context was through the unity of the "representor" (not the represented), Kierkegaard sees this unification as merely *external*. He sees Christendom (bourgeois society) as characterized by a dialectic which parallels the Hobbesian logic:

> . . . the majority sees itself in its representative and is set free by the consciousness that it is the majority which it represented, in a sort of self-consciousness. (*Present Age*, p. 52)

But if people see *themselves* in their representation, what does representation mean?

Kierkegaard raises the question which he thinks has no answer:

> . . . in the end the whole generation has become a representation, who represent . . . it is difficult to say *who*. (p. 45)

This problem of the loss of the subjective element (that it is difficult to say "who" is doing anything) in the process of representation (comparable to Rousseau's idea that the will cannot be represented) is for Kierkegaard the problem of "leveling." The process of leveling is the "victory of abstraction over the individual," the workings of an "abstract power" (*Present Age*, p. 52). In belonging to an abstraction, people "band together in cases where it is an absolute contradiction to be more than one" (p. 53). Abstract equality (leveling) has no personal relation to any individual but rather is "an abstract relationship which is the same for every one" (p. 57). Abstraction culminates in the victory of the "public" which is "a phantom, its spirit a monstrous abstraction, an all-embracing something which is nothing, a mirage" (p. 59). But this mirage is also a mirror, for it is through the mirror of the public that the process of leveling, the process of "reflection" takes place. Reflection is the prison of envy:

> . . . the idea of reflection is . . . envy, and it is therefore twofold in its action: it is selfish within the individual and it results in the selfishness of the society around

him, which thus works against him. . . . The envy which
springs from reflection imprisons man's will and his
strength . . . he finds himself in the vast prison formed
by the reflection of those around him. (*Present Age*,
p. 48)

Reflection is the "hardest creditor in existence" (p. 58). Through
its selfish envy it "makes such demands upon the individual that
by asking too much it prevents him from doing anything" (p. 48).
Accordingly, individuals aspire "to be nothing at all—in order to
become the public" (p. 64). What would the public look like if it
were personified? Kierkegaard tries to imagine:

. . . one of the Roman emperors, a large well-fed figure,
suffering from boredom, looking only for the sensual
intoxication of laughter. . . . And so for a change he
wanders about, indolent rather than bad, but with a
negative desire to dominate. (*Present Age*, p. 56)

All relationships in the present age tend toward this image:
there is no parental authority, no conflict between father and
child, just polite, indifferent behavior. The relation between parent and child becomes "irreproachable, for it is really in the process of ceasing to exist" (*Present Age*, p. 44). Abstract indifference
replaces concrete relationship. But concrete relationship is necessarily what Kierkegaard calls a personal relationship of "domination": the child's obedience to the father, the "admiration of the
subject . . . which gives recognized importance to the master" (p.
45). Thus what the present age has achieved is the transcendence
of concrete experiences of "dominion" (or possession), which become instead an abstract and generalized dominance. Relationships, if they are to be concrete, must be those of master and slave,
and the present age blurs the distinction, creates, in the Hegelian
phrase, masters without slaves and slaves without masters. In the
ambiguity of this situation, what is needed is the recreation of the
logic of feudal property relations, in the interior of the personality.
What is needed is one's own "feudal castle," which in its inwardness "makes the fetters of dependence and the crown of dominion
light" (p. 45). What is needed is for the individual to "be content
with himself," to learn, "instead of dominating others" (which is
impossible since there are no possibilities for concrete relations of
dominion left in the present age), "to dominate himself, content as

priest to be his own audience, as author his own reader" (p. 57). What is needed is self-possession and freedom from others as the "hardest creditor."

To put this differently: for Kierkegaard the significant characteristic of relatedness is that it is possessed whole, that there are no partial, contingent loose ends. This outlook emerges clearly in his understanding of the experience of guilt. Guilt for Kierkegaard was the "decisive expression for the existential pathos" (*Postscript*, pp. 468-469). The consciousness of guilt expresses the relationship of an existing individual to an "external happiness" and without this relationship, Kierkegaard thought, one would never conceive of himself as "totally or essentially guilty" (p. 471). This absolute relationship to an eternal happiness is, for Kierkegaard, absolute

> . . . precisely for the fact that one possesses it as one's own by relating oneself to the absolute, as a jewel which can be possessed whole and cannot be parcelled out in small change. (*Postscript*, p. 481)

The pathos of guilt is that it is unmediated. Were guilt capable of being mediated or relieved, this would mean that guilt was an external determinant:

> Mediation dispenses man from absorbing himself in determinants of totality and makes him busy outwardly, his guilt being external. . . ." (*Postscript*, p. 481)

[The idea that guilt never has an "external occasion," that freedom toward guilt is one's own possibility, is developed in Kierkegaard's *Dread*, pp. 97-98.] That is, essential guilt would be simple debt. But guilt is *one's own*, is possessed whole. Guilt is one's own debt, the capital in oneself:

> . . . the beginning must be made by becoming guilty and from that moment increasing the total capital guilt by a new guilt at a usurious rate of interest. (*Postscript*, p. 469)

Kierkegaard compares the consciousness of guilt to the gold standard; without it men are bankrupt:

> Just as paper money may be important as a means of

exchange between man and man, but is in itself a
chimerical entity in case there is in the last resort no
gold reserve to support it, so, too, . . . the conventional,
the external, the legal conception of the ethical may be
useful enough in common intercourse, but in case it is
forgotten that the substantial value of the ethical must be
in the inwardness of the individual, . . . in case a whole
generation could forget this . . . that generation is . . .
ethically impoverished in an essential sense, and is
essentially bankrupt. (*Postscript*, p. 486)

In his journals Kierkegaard expresses a sense of complete indebtedness to
God which he thinks is completely consistent with freedom and independence: it is ". . . to him who made me independent, while he neverthe-
less retained everything, that I owe all things." See *Journals*, p. 114. This is
the only "debt" which matters.

The interpenetration of the language of guilt and the logic of
capital, the relationship between debt and guilt, is a theme we
will return to explicitly below. Though Kierkegaard himself
thought that guilt consciousness was less an attribute of existence
than what he called "sin consciousness," the emphasis on essential guilt as definitive of authenticity is the most important contribution that Kierkegaard makes to the tradition of authentic
self-possession in the modern West. Here I will turn to the development of these themes, to the relationship between authenticity
and possession, in Heidegger's *Being and Time*.

Heidegger: Guilt and Debt, Authenticity and Property

The Kierkegaardian legacy of the essential inwardness of guilt and
therefore the concern to distinguish external, inessential debt from
primordial ontological guilt, is fully developed in Heidegger's *Being
and Time*. I begin this section on Heidegger with a discussion of the
relationship between guilt and debt both because I think it crucial to
an understanding of the political psychology implicit in *Being and
Time* and because I think that this psychology is most characteristic
of the experience of *extasis*. Heidegger, I want to argue, desituates
guilt from the context of indebtedness in which it has meaning.

Heidegger contends, to the contrary, that authenticity "calls us forth
into the situation" through what he calls "resoluteness." The "they" is

irresolute and knows only what Heidegger calls the "general situation," a "mixture of circumstances and accidents," those "opportunities" which are "closest to it." One aspect of the "untruth" of this general situation is its commonsensical understanding of conscience as indebtedness. Resoluteness "appropriates untruth authentically"; ". . . the situation *is* only through resoluteness and in it." Resoluteness appropriates indebtedness, in other words, as *its own*, taking the burden of the "general situation" on itself through its guilt. But this is precisely what I mean by "desituation": the transformation of circumstances of indebtedness which are "closest" to us into essential guilt. It is in this sense that I use the word *desituation* throughout this section. See *Being and Time*, H299-300 for Heidegger's discussion.

The question which Heidegger wants to ask with respect to the nature of guilt is: "What does it mean *to be* guilty?" not "What are the circumstances of guilt?" or "In what situations, in terms of what concrete relationships to others, is guilt experienced?" The ontological analysis of guilt begins, for Heidegger, with the inauthentic "everyday interpretation," the "commonsense" understanding of guilt. Of this way of beginning, Heidegger says, ". . . wherever we see something wrongly, some injunction as to the primordial 'idea' of the phenomenon is revealed along with it" (*Being and Time*, H281).

Heidegger suggests that the first criterion of the existential meaning of guilt is that "Guilty!" is, commonly, a predicate for the "I am" (*Being and Time*, H281). In emphasizing the "I am" of guilt, Heidegger focuses on the *individuating* aspect of the commonsense experiences of guilt rather than upon the common contexts within which guilt is attributed. Yet it is apparent that Heidegger understands these contexts to be defined by indebtedness. He describes two related aspects of everyday relations of indebtedness which ordinary expressions of guilt reflect:

> (1) Being-guilty in the sense of owing or having "something due on account," where one is to "give back to the other something to which the latter has claim." Being-guilty as "having debts" in this sense is related to other modes of concern for others, e.g., "depriving, borrowing, withholding, taking, stealing—failing to satisfy, in some way or other, the claims which others have made as to their possessions." (*Being and Time*, H281)
> (2) Having debts (and responsibility) come together as a definite kind of behavior, as "making oneself responsible." This can mean making oneself punishable

by breaking a law having to do with debts, but it need not be "related to anyone's possessions." That is, the requirement "which one fails to satisfy" can "regulate the very manner in which we are with one another publicly." As such it has the character of "coming to owe something to others," not simply through breaking a law, but as well "through my having the responsibility for the other's becoming endangered in his existence, led astray, or even ruined." (*Being and Time*, H282)

In general, being-guilty in the commonsense view of "having come to owe something to another" is defined by Heidegger as

> *Being-the-basis* for a lack of something in . . . an other. . . . This kind of lacking is a failure to satisfy some requirement which applies to one's existent being with others." (*Being and Time*, H282)

Heidegger here describes a matrix of indebtedness, "economic" in both the narrow sense of particular relationships of exchange (withholding, borrowing, stealing, and the like) and in the broad sense of a public manner of life which might accurately be called "social" indebtedness, that is, owing something *to others*. Directly after this description, Heidegger comments that "[we] need not consider how such requirements arise and in what way their character as requirements and laws must be conceived by reason of their having such a source" (*Being and Time*, H282).

This lack of historical perspective in Heidegger has been criticized by Adorno, who has remarked that the transformation of concrete socioeconomic relationships into ontological attributes of being human "transforms a bad empirical reality into a transcendence." This is what Adorno means when he says:

> The jargon of authenticity, which sells self-identity as something higher, projects the exchange formula onto that which imagines that it is not exchangeable. . . ." (*Jargon*, p. 76)

My purpose here is to demonstrate the way in which the logic of exchange relationships of private property is implicit in Heidegger's conception of authenticity.

The origin of the matrix of indebtedness which defines the commonsense view of guilt is, for Heidegger, irrelevant with respect to the project of determining its ontological character. Hence the "ordinary phenomena of 'guilt' which are related to our concernful being with others," Heidegger says, "will *drop out*" in an ontological analysis of guilt (*Being and Time*, H283). This matrix of indebtedness would be the basis for a *political* theory of guilt or for a historical analysis of the genesis of these relationships. But this is not Heidegger's concern; rather he argues that essential, ontological guilt is *prior* to debt:

> . . . being-guilty does not first result from an
> indebtedness, but . . . on the contrary, indebtedness
> becomes possible only "on the basis" of a primordial
> being-guilty. (*Being and Time*, H284)

Here Heidegger reverses Nietzsche. By placing the phenomenon of guilt in history and relating it to experiences of powerlessness, Nietzsche situates guilt in a context defined essentially by relationships of indebtedness.

In bracketing out the possibilities of a political/historical perspective on the phenomenon of guilt, Heidegger is concerned that where guilt is misunderstood, where it is reduced to debt, then the timeless, essential call of conscience, the call of "Guilty!," can be avoided. Authentic guilt might then be "thrust aside into the domain of concern in the sense of reckoning up claims and balancing them off." Rather than root the meaning of guilt in the contingent everyday socioeconomic context of indebtedness, we must learn, if we are to live authentically, "to conceive the idea of 'Guilty!' in terms of Dasein's kind of being" (H283). For Heidegger, authentic *Dasein* ("being-there" in the sense of the individuating apprehension that *I am*) is possible only if guilt is an essential characteristic of being human.

Wherever guilt is understood as a "lack," "when something which ought to be and which can be is missing" (H283), it takes on the character, for Heidegger, of a thing (the "present-at-hand"), and presence-at-hand is not Dasein's being. Rather, Dasein is the basis of what Heidegger calls "nullity" (*Nichtigkeit*): that is, it has as its possibility *not being* its authentic self, of being *in*authentic (H285). This nullity is prior to the experience of indebtedness, and it is not a "lack": it is rather what Heidegger calls the "structure of thrownness," that situation of "not having chosen the others and one's not being able to choose them" (H285).

Dasein *is guilty* because it is not itself, and because it has not-being-itself as its *own* possibility. The essential call of conscience brings Dasein "back to itself from its lostness in the 'they'" (H287). Everyday Dasein is "so absorbed in the 'they'" that it has allowed its authentic possibilities to be presented to it "by the way in which the 'they' has publicly interpreted things" (H270). This context of public interpretation is the matrix of social indebtedness.

In the world of its concern, Dasein can lose itself; it can be "taken over," absorbed and possessed:

> When Dasein is absorbed in the world of its
> concern—that is, at the same time, in its being-with
> toward others—it is not itself. *Who* is it, then, who has
> taken over being as everyday being-with-one-another?
> (H125)

Heidegger's answer to this question is "the they." It is out of the experience of "belonging to the they" that the call of conscience calls men to their authentic possibilities.

The logic of the "they" is a straightforward extension of Kierkegaard's conception of the "public." The everyday experience of identity, Heidegger argues, is not the experience of "I" in the sense of "my own self" but in the sense of the "they self": others take away the being of Dasein, which is in "subjection" to them. But these others are not definite others. "One belongs to the others oneself and enhances their power"; it is the power of the neuter "they" which is enhanced, not you or him or "some people" (H126).

Perhaps the most significant aspect of being lost in the "they" is that the "they" tranquilizes Dasein as to the certain fact of its own death:

> The "they" does not permit us the courage for anxiety in
> the face of death. (H254)

The anticipation of one's own death, like the call of conscience, brings Dasein to itself. Heidegger emphasizes that this anticipation, like the essential call "Guilty!," is characteristically individuating. Death, one's "ownmost possibility" is "nonrelational" for Heidegger in the sense that "all being-with-others . . . will fail us when our ownmost potentiality for being is the issue" (H 264). In this sense,

> The nonrelational character of death, as understood in anticipation, individualizes Dasein down to itself. (H264)

To recapitulate: everyday Dasein is lost in the they; one common misunderstanding from within this lostness is that guilt is indebtedness to others; another is that only "some people" die, and therefore everyday Dasein is fleeing in the face of death. Both essential guilt and the anticipation of death individualize Dasein. Guilt and death, to put it differently, are essentially *idiotic:* experiences which signify separation from, nonrelation to, others.

Heidegger is quite clear that this nonrelationality does not mean that Dasein is *essentially* nonrelational or idiotic. The fact that others are no help in facing my death, that "they" cannot die my death for me, does not imply that the structures of being-with-others must be excluded from authentic being-oneself. Being-alongside and solicitous being-with are "essential to Dasein's constitution":

> Dasein is authentically itself only to the extent that *as*
> concernful being-alongside and solicitous being-with, it
> projects itself upon its ownmost potentiality-for-being
> rather than upon the possibility of the they self. (H263)

Here Heidegger presents the movement of authentic freedom toward one's death (like the call of "Guilty!") as wrenching the self away from the "they," and as making authentic concern for others possible. This movement, however, is possible for Dasein only by virtue of experiencing a nonrelational perspective: that one is deprived of all relation to others in death. From that perspective one learns that one is related to others authentically only *on the basis* of separation. The ontological analysis of guilt and death teach this lesson. Heidegger emphasizes the connection between the ideas of authenticity and nonrelationality in his discussion of the call of conscience: understanding the call "Guilty!" is ". . . more authentic the more nonrelationally Dasein hears and understands *its* own being-appealed-to, the less the meaning of the call gets perverted by what one says or by what is fitting and accepted" (H280).

There is, therefore, a fundamental contrast in Heidegger between that which is appropriate or fitting (*Geeignetheit*) and that which is authentic. When one is lost, absorbed, or indebted to others (lost in the they) one is misled by what *they* think is appropriate. To behave appropriately (to act in terms of the "they") is to behave *as if* one were a thing, as if one could *be appropriated* by others. Heidegger argues that "the ontological structure designated by the term 'property' is that of some definite character which it is possible for things to possess" (H83). "Property" can be an attribute only of things which can be *essentially* appropriate. In what I take to be one of the most central passages in *Being and Time*, Heidegger distinguishes the character of "property":

> [Dasein] comports itself toward its being as its ownmost
> possibility. In each case Dasein *is* its possibility, and it
> "has" this possibility, but not just as a property
> [*eigenschaftlich*], as something present-at-hand would.
> And because Dasein is in each case essentially its own
> possibility, it *can*, in its very being, "choose" itself and
> win itself; it can also lose itself and never win itself; or
> only "seem" to do so. But only in so far as it is
> essentially something which can be *authentic*
> [*eigentlich*]—that is, something of its own [*eigen*]—can it
> have lost itself and not yet won itself. As modes of
> being, authenticity and inauthenticity (these expressions
> have been chosen terminologically in the strict sense)
> are both grounded in the fact that any Dasein
> whatsoever is characterized by mineness [*Jemeinigkeit*].
> (H42-43)

The etymological root of Heidegger's key terminology is systematically property-related. Both "authenticity" and "appropriateness" are rooted in the German *eigen*, one's own. The alternatives which Dasein has as *its own* are either to lose itself in appropriateness, to become alienated from itself, from its individuality (inauthenticity), or to take itself back from lostness in the "they," to become that unique "property" relationship which only human being can be, to become not *Eigenschaft* (property) but *eigentlich* (authentic). Thus the taking back or reappropriating of oneself as *one's own* property through the call of conscience and the anticipation of death establishes the logic of property as a relation of the self to itself and to others: one either possesses oneself (not as a "thing" but nonetheless as something which can be one's own) or one is possessed by the "they." The possibilities of winning or losing oneself, possessing oneself or being-possessed by the "they" are, I think constitutive of the central tension in Heidegger's work. The emphasis upon the idiocy of the essential movements of authenticity, on the need to reappropriate what has been appropriated (and it *must* have been appropriated for it to be *re*appropriated) sheds light on the distinction which Heidegger draws between debt and guilt. Debt can, I think, accurately be understood to represent the common experience of everyday relationships of inauthenticity, where being-possessed by the "they" defines the self at-a-loss, "lacking" itself and depending upon anonymous "others" for its sense of self. If one were to view this dependence in fundamentally materialist terms, one could break it down into concrete relationships of economic and emotional dependence, relationships between husbands and wives, employers and employees, parents and children—each with its characteristic modality of indebtedness. But Heidegger does not take this view, for taking it would be to take the context of indebtedness as primary. Rather, I would suggest, Heidegger transforms the logic of this everyday context into an ontology of guilt and death, arguing that authenticity *per se* has nothing to do with the historical nexus of relationships which define the common situation within which Dasein finds itself.

It is clearly true that we do not "choose" the others, that we are "thrown" into the world with others. But that world is not abstract and anonymous: it may be distinguished by relationships of domination, danger, and indebtedness, along the dimensions of social and economic class, gradations of prestige, wealth, and the like. But authenticity is the same for the beggar and the banker: one *can* be one's own despite the context of social, economic, and political indebtedness. Though it seems clear that Heidegger's ultimate concern is with the possibility of authentic *relationships* with others, such relationships are possible only to the extent to which *individual* Dasein, confronting the depth of its idiocy, establishes this idiocy as the basis of its authentic possibilities. This idiocy, I want to suggest, is not logically entailed by what Heidegger takes as the most definitely individuative experience of anticipating one's death: one might reasonably argue that death, far from being one's *ownmost* certainty, is that which is most certainly *common* to all. The anticipation of death would then become simply a *species* trait. This is, I think, the direction of Marx's comment that "death seems to be a harsh victory of the species over the particular individual and to contradict the species' unity, but the particular individual is only a particular *generic being*, and as such mortal" (*Young Marx*, p. 307). The choice between these perspectives on death is never discussed by Heidegger. Rather, I think, the focus on essential individuation as the prerequisite for authentic relations is dictated by the contingencies of a context which defines alternatives of relatedness in possessive ways.

In the course of continuing to trace the tradition of authenticity to its culmination in Sartre, it will be clear that Sartre defines contingency as the mode of possession. This definition is, I think, *implicit* in Heidegger, and along with the Kierkegaardian emphasis on essential guilt, it defines the persistence of the assumptions of the possessive unconscious as the underlying logic of authenticity. Apart from this logic, the need to reappropriate a self which has been taken hold of by others is unintelligible.

We have seen in Rousseau the basis for the concern to overcome the need of others; we have seen in Kierkegaard the defensive metaphor of the feudal castle of the self which, for modern man, accomplishes this purpose; in Heidegger we have seen the logic of transcending indebtedness toward ontological guilt; we have now to examine the ways in which Sartre draws this tradition to its culmination.

Sartre: Contingency and Possession — The Third Ekstasis

> ... we apprehend our inapprehensible being-for-others in the form of a *possession*. I am possessed by the other; ... the other holds a secret—the secret of what I am. He makes me and thereby he possesses me, and this possession is nothing other than the consciousness of possessing me. (*Being and Nothingness*, p. 364)

For Sartre, there are what he calls three *"ekstases"* which characterize being human, three experiences in which the self is separated from, stands out from, itself. The first is that of temporality, in terms of which human being is "being what it is not and not being what it is," that is, suspended between future and past. The second is that of reflection, in which the self takes itself as its own object. The third *ekstasis* is that of "being-for-others," in which the self experiences itself as a self which it is, but which it cannot get hold of. The problem of the third *ekstasis* is the problem of Tantalus:

I want to stretch out my hand and grab hold of this being

which is presented to me as *my being* but at a distance—like the dinner of Tantalus; I want to found it by my very freedom. For if in one sense my being-as-object is an unbearable contingency and the pure "possession" of myself by another, still in another sense this being stands as the indication of what I should be obliged to recover and found in order to be the foundation of myself. But this is conceivable only if I assimilate the other's freedom. Thus my project of recovering myself is fundamentally a project of absorbing the other. (*Being and Nothingness*, p. 364)

The identification of contingency and possession means for Sartre that in the very structure of being-for-others, in the experience of being seen, judged, and interpreted by others, in the very presence of others, there is enslavement. The slavery which is the necessary experience of others is not, for Sartre, capable of being surmounted:

... this slavery is not a historical result ... I am a slave to the degree that my being is dependent at the center of a freedom which is not mine and which is the very condition of my being. ... In so far as I am the instrument of possibilities which are not my possibilities ... I am *in danger*. This danger is not an accident but the permanent structure of my being-for-others. (*Being and Nothingness*, p. 268)

One of Sartre's most interesting formulations of the relationship between consciousness and possession is his short essay "Une Idée Fondamental de la Phénoménologie de Husserl: l'Intentionalité" (*Situations I*). There he criticizes what he calls the "digestive" or "alimentary" philosophy of both empiricism and neo-Kantianism from the perspective of Husserl's conception of intentionality. He takes as his point of departure for the essay the phrase "Il la mangeait des yeux" (he devoured her with his eyes) and comments that this phrase reflects "the illusion common to both realism and idealism that to know is to eat." He argues that "... consciousness cannot, without dishonesty, liken itself to possession." Thus his attack on what he calls *la philosophie alimentaire* posits a conception of consciousness which is not limited to "knowing," where knowing is understood to be some form of possession, assimilation, or eating of the known object. In this sense Husserl, by emphasizing that consciousness exists as always consciousness *of* something other than self (intentionality), restores, Sartre thinks, "the world of artists and prophets," a "frightful, hostile and dangerous" world, but one with "havens of grace and love." (All translations are mine.) In *Being and Nothingness*, however, danger is consistently identified with the danger of being-possessed, absorbed, assimilated, or eaten by others. There Sartre refers to the totality of the images of "violation by sight" as the "Actaeon complex" and says directly that "To know is to devour with the eyes" (p. 587). Here he is more thoroughly Hegelian in his assumptions, noting as he does in several following passages that for Hegel, "desire is the desire of devouring." Hence the quality of "being-possessed" means "to be for someone" (*être à*) and the bond of possession is "an internal bond of being" (p. 588), that is, it has ontological status. It is difficult to see in this either the "dishonesty" or the "illusion" to which Sartre refers in *Situations I*.

For the others to be the "alienation of my possibilities" entails a special understanding of the nature of human freedom: man's free project is for Sartre the project of possessing the world. The symbol which Sartre chooses to express the project of human possibility is that of God, and "possibility is the possibility of appropriating" (*Being and Nothingness*, p. 589). Man in the face of the notion of God (enslaved by the metaphor of the master) is characterized by insufficiency of being (the "for-itself") attempting to become God (the "in-itself"). To be in the world is therefore to form the project of "possessing the world" (p. 597): man is condemned to appropriate that which is always fleeing from him. There is no better example of this futility than the contradiction of attempting to seek the "possibility" of transcending the limits of possession, and it is in this light that Sartre calls man a "useless passion."

The consciousness of man strives, Sartre maintains, for "impermeability and infinite density." This project of becoming its own foundation Sartre calls "the withdrawal to found being," that internal relation of the for-itself to the in-itself which Sartre calls "ownership" (p. 588). This internal relationship implies for Sartre that "the desire to be is always accompanied by the desire to have (p. 597). Possessive consciousness thus defines its relation to the world as that of ownership, and impermeability is its absolute value. Since, however, "possession is an enterprise which death always renders still unachieved" (pp. 592-593), being is always beyond our grasp, always fleeing from us, though freedom is possession.

The other is present when one experiences that freedom fleeing from one:

> Thus suddenly an object has appeared which has stolen the world from me. (p. 255)

Taken in the strict philosophical sense, this *ekstasis*, like the others, defines man as a "lack of being." But taken in a broader sense, Sartre's demand that the project of recovering oneself is the project of absorbing the other reveals Sartre's philosophy as a way of life, a way of responding to the "danger" which contingency poses. Merleau-Ponty, treating the question of Hegel's "existentialism," notes but does not develop the import of this perspective, in a discussion of the Hegelian conception of absolute knowledge:

> Absolute knowledge ... wherein consciousness at last becomes equal to its spontaneous life and regains its self-possession, is perhaps not a philosophy but a way of life. (*Sense*, p. 64)

Hegel's thought is existentialist, Merleau-Ponty argues,

> ... in that it views man not as being from the start a consciousness in full possession of its own clear thoughts but as a life which is its own responsibility and which tries to understand itself. All of *The Phenomenology of Mind* describes man's efforts to reappropriate himself. (p. 65)

To say that the human understanding reappropriates itself in the struggle for self-possession as a way of life is to invoke the logic of the possessive unconscious: it is to say that one's freedom always entails possession. Sartre states that the goal of what he calls "existential psychoanalysis" is to grasp the *meaning* of human choice, of freedom; freedom for that being which is the lack of being is the "choice of being," "either directly or by appropriation of the world, or rather by both at once" (*Being and Nothingness*, p. 599). Choice, then, is necessarily "behavioral," about possession. What existentialist psychoanalysis reveals is the concrete projects through which man chooses his being. "It remains to explain," Sartre notes, "why I choose to possess the world through *this* particular object rather than another. We shall reply that here we see the peculiar character of human freedom" (p. 599).

I would respond by saying that here we see the peculiar limits of the logic of the possessive unconscious: that freedom is necessarily understood as the choice among possessive modes of life; that "authentic" freedom is but one of the possible possessive alternatives, the one which achieves self-possession; that this authenticity [Though Sartre does not utilize the term *authenticité* in his work, the idea is implicit in his discussion of freedom.] derives its meaning as "a defense against others" (p. 592); that it is a compensation for the threat which personal dependence offers, when defined as the experience of being-possessed by others.

Thus a philosophy which begins with the assumption that man is an emptiness without content, a nothingness (p. lxvi), is compensatory. Possession is a compensation for emptiness, and the emptiest of lives are those which are related by separation, or as Sartre puts it, which are characterized by a "primary absence of relation," wherein there is, between the other and myself, "a nothingness of separation" (p. 230).

Sartrean freedom thus takes as its given the experience of possession as definitive of the *meaning* of human possibility. The relational, the contingent, become subsumed under the category of possession, as the inauthentic experience of being-possessed. An authentically free choice chooses the construct of the Kierkegaardian feudal castle, within which it can hear clearly the Heideggerian call of "Guilty!" That call is experienced as if the self were what Schopenhauer called "a madman shut up in an impregnable blockhouse." Sartre, in discussing this quotation (Schopenhauer's description of the solipsist) does not seem to understand that his own response to it is precisely applicable to the tradition of authentic self-possession which he brings to a culmination: "What a confession of impotence" (p. 229).

The cry of "Guilty!" is the confession of one who has *taken all there is to take* upon himself—the emptiness, the absence of meaningful relationships, the despair of behavioral possibilities—who becomes his own possession because freedom resides not in whether or not one accepts the possessive framework of meaning, but in *how* one accepts it. All else, from this perspective, is either meaningless or dangerous.

The helplessness and powerlessness of this situation is for Sartre an expression of primordial guilt:

> Thus original sin is my upsurge in a world where there
> are others; and whatever may be my further relations
> with others, these relations will be only variations on the
> original theme of my guilt. (p. 410)

In order to understand this perspective more thoroughly, it is necessary to examine in some detail the psychology and philosophy of powerlessness which it expresses.

5
Self-Possession and the Estrangement of Power: The American Example

The very framework of modern society confines [people] to projects not their own, but from every side, such changes now press upon the men and women of the mass society, who accordingly feel that they are without purpose in an epoch in which they are without power. (C. Wright Mills, *Power Elite*, p. 3)

Authenticity, I have argued, is a defense against contingency and dependence, understood as being-possessed by others. Identity, torn between possessive alternatives, is in this sense a scarce good, perpetually vacillating between authentic and inauthentic possibilities, where authenticity represents the struggle to constantly "reappropriate" one's being as it flees from one. The tradition of authenticity presents us with a schizophrenic vision of the world, in which idiocy is the prerequisite of authenticity. Idiocy thus becomes descriptive of the separation of the self and the other across an unbridgeable gap of powerlessness, an excluded middle: there is nothing beyond the self but a "medley of other things," undifferentiated and anonymous.

This schizophrenic vision articulates one extreme of the dilemma of the possessive unconscious: that of an intense subjectivism, what Emerson called the "infinitude of the private man," withdrawn from relationships, beyond the need of others. This perspective depends on the assumption that all relationships are necessarily relationships of dependence, and that dependence entails being indebted to or possessed by some other. The logic of the possessive unconscious is such that its dichotomous alternatives, possess or be-possessed, admit only that freedom which replaces indebtedness to others by indebtedness to oneself alone. Authentic self-possession reconciles the "problem" of dependence by taking the logic of indebtedness upon the self, by internalizing this logic. If all relationships are assumed to entail indebtedness, and thus to threaten the loss of power and control, then power within this field of powerlessness demands the transformation of indebtedness into a relation of the self to itself. This transformation does not transcend the logic of possession; rather, it incorporates it as the authentic possibility of the self.

The authenticity tradition in America begins with the nineteenth-century Transcendentalists. Emerson is the American Rousseau, and John Adams and James Madison are the central spokesmen for two parts of the Hobbesian position. Adams articulates the notion of an identity which is essentially dependent on others; Madison expresses the logic of institutions designed to separate and prevent human combination. Both taken together present a picture of precisely the abstract dependence on "society" which Emerson and Thoreau find so destructive. Society was for Madison and Adams a field of interacting forces which always entails the processes of debt, credit, and separation. The anxieties of this framework of inevitability lead to the Transcendentalist attempt to achieve some power over a world defined in terms of indebtedness. As we have seen above with the European tradition of authenticity, these attempts involve the interiorization of the logic of indebtedness (and as well, of the Madisonian logic of separation), the rejection of a politics defined as external indebtedness, and a resumption of this very politics as a relation of the self to itself. Thus the conversation between Madison and Adams on the one side and the Transcendentalists on the other represents the American example of the modern neurosis, the meaning of which is deeply rooted in the possessive unconscious.

In order to appreciate the depth of these roots, we must first explore the nature of the Hobbesian assumptions and the plight of the desperate debtor in America.

Spectemur Agendo: John Adams

Adams is usually referred to as the American "realist," a sort of

Machiavelli in America. The nature of what has been called his realism is his conception of human history as the history of class struggle, a cyclical battle between the extremities of wealth and poverty. History was, in other words, the working out of the antagonism between creditors and debtors. For Adams, over the melancholy course of this history it really did not matter which faction emerged as dominant: the result was the same in every society, as he put it, where property existed. To mix both factions in a deliberative body was to facilitate either oligarchy or tyranny:

> In every society where property exists, there will ever
> be a struggle between rich and poor. Mixed in one
> assembly, *equal laws* can never be expected. They will
> either be made by the numbers, to plunder the few who
> are rich, or by influence, to fleece the many who are
> poor. (*Political Writings*, p. 158)

Though property was, Adams said, as sacred as the laws of God, its institution among men was not by nature. Rather:

> Indolence is the natural character of man to such a
> degree that nothing but the necessities of hunger, thirst,
> and other wants equally pressing can stimulate him to
> action, until education is introduced in civilized
> societies and the strongest motives of ambition to excel
> in arts, trades, and professions are established in the
> minds of all men. Until this emulation is introduced, the
> lazy savage holds property in too little estimation to give
> himself trouble for the preservation or acquisition of it.
> (p. 148)

Emulation, then, is the principle of civilization. Coterminous with the establishment of property is its defense and covetousness. Since the majority are without property but covet it, all debtors are potentially destructive of property rights. If all were to be decided by popular vote, Adams continued,

> . . . the time would not be long before . . . pretexts
> [would] be invented by degrees to countenance the
> majority in dividing all the property among them, or at
> least in sharing it equally with its present possessors.
> Debts would be abolished first. (p. 148)

Nature, though it did not establish property, did in Adams's outlook establish the passions which would make the struggle over property characteristic of civil society. The most fundamental passion in this regard was what Adams called the "passion for distinction," from which emulation, ambition, jealousy, and envy are derivative—educated expressions of its logic. Adams defines this passion in the following way:

> A desire to be observed, considered, esteemed, praised, beloved, and admired by [one's] fellows. (p. 178)

That passion, then, is for what Hegel called "recognition," the desire of the desire of others, what Adams saw as the desire to be "seen, heard, talked of, approved and respected" by those about one, and was definitive of human need. Concern for the "esteem of others" was for Adams so significant that it was "the principle end of government to regulate this passion, which in its turn becomes a principle means of government." The passion for distinction was for Adams "the only adequate instrument of order and subordination in society" (p. 178). It was, as well, the principal source of human despair:

> It sooner and oftener produces despair and a detestation of existence of equal importance to individuals, to families and to nations. (p. 178)

Yet the passion for distinction drove men, Adams thought, to the highest expressions of their nature, the ability to act "for the good of others." He chose the Latin motto *"Spectemur agendo"* ("Let us be watched in the doing") as the root of this ability. The poor man, for Adams, suffered not material deprivation, but the deprivation of not being seen: "He is not disapproved, censured or reproached; he is only not seen" (p. 183). To escape this deprivation was the work of the passion of distinction, and Adams envisioned a society in which the principle would operate so that all people constantly struggled up toward the light, where they could be seen:

> . . . every citizen in the commonwealth is constantly struggling for a better rank, that he may draw the observation of more eyes. (p. 185)

This early American conception of the search for better rank, the drive upward for admiration, love, and recognition based on the validation of one's identity by and through others, is in this sense the instrument of order and subordination in society. But as Adams saw, this passionate search for esteem is infinite in its need: so long as this need dominates human activity, identity is never secure, there is always the despairing doubt that one is not really *there* unless others are watching. It is this despair that leads Thoreau, as I will argue below, to cry: Damn your eyes!

What John Winthrop had said about the American Puritan's "City on a Hill," namely that "the eyes of all people are upon us" (Miller, ed., *Puritans*, p. 83), is by Adams extended to the logic of individual psychology. But the legacy of the experience of being watched is, for the individual, the experience of either infinite worthlessness or paranoia: that I am worthless unless others are watching or that the others are always "talking about me." Both of these consequences of the desire for esteem (despair and paranoia) are rooted in the psychology of indebtedness. If the self is indebted to others, or to some generalized principle of estima-tion for its sense of self, then there is a terror about dependence on others. The American Transcendentalists accepted the equa-tion of other-directedness and indebtedness as the essence of "so-ciety," but rejected this preoccupation with public esteem as inau-thentic. In the process, however, they rejected the possibility of meaningful social and political relationships altogether. This is testimony to how deeply imbedded is the assumption that societal interaction is necessarily the experience of indebtedness, that there are no other meaningful conceptions of the experience of social contingency, that there is no authentic alternative save withdrawal from "society." But in order to understand the terror of public esteem we must see what that society looks like in which despair and paranoia are constant threats. As we shall see, Tocqueville understood that public esteem was an abstraction superimposed upon social fragmentation. We must first note that this was precisely what James Madison assumed to be the most natural and beneficial form of society.

The Logic of Separation: Madison

The central preoccupation of Madison's political theory was to maintain the principle that the authority of government is based in society, while avoiding the consequences of this principle, which were, for Madison, the diseases of instability, injustice, and confusion. Madison suggested that the federal republic exemplified a method of coping with this dilemma:

> Whilst all authority in it will be derived from and dependent on the society, the society itself will be broken into so many parts, interests and classes of citizens, that the rights of individuals, or the minority will be in little danger from interested combinations of the majority. (*Federalist Papers*, p. 324)

The "broken" society, society characterized by fragmentation, division, and separation of its parts, was for Madison the prerequisite of political stability. Anarchy in this view means unity, unity means oppression: injustice in the "combination" of an interested majority (p. 324). Thus what people share is separation. The study of politics, like the study of nature or the human mind, was necessarily a science built upon the principles of boundary and separation. The "delineations of nature" (vegetable vs. unorganized life), like the distinct mental faculties (judgment, desire, volition, and the like), were boundaries which were discoverable in the natural sciences. Human institutions, the fruit of a mind divided, obey for Madison the same logic of separation.

Alexander Hamilton expressed the permanence of this logic of separation in his argument that the maxims of ethics and politics were nearly as clear as the principles of nature. As in nature, order—the logic of separation—is to be discovered and described as implicit in human activity, not to be created. Thus for Madison and Hamilton there are principles in all sciences—including the science of politics—which demand the assent of reason. Even the "abstruse paradoxes" of geometry, the principle of, for example, "the infinite divisibility of finite matter" can be accepted by the human mind (*Federalist Papers*, p. 194). Unfortunately, as Hobbes had noted much earlier in his exploration of the relation between the principles of geometry and those of politics, men are in Hamilton's words "less tractable" where politics is concerned than where paradoxes are "abstruse." When this "untractableness" gets carried too far, Hamilton notes, it degenerates into "obstinacy and perverseness."

With respect to the political paradox at the core of the Madisonian position, that anarchy is unity and separation is what we share, substantively different conceptions of these relationships become not alternatives, but rather unreasonable, obstinate, perverse, or disingenuous positions. Those who do not compromise, who do not bargain, balance, separate, or disperse, who are not persuaded that justice is balance among factions which constitute societal fragmentation, are, in short, irrational.

Here the Burkean conception of political reason, which Paine characterized as an "astrological, mysterious" conception, is at the core of Madison. Burke put it this way:

> The rights of man in government are their advantages;
> and these are often in balances between differences of
> good; and in compromises between good and evil, and
> sometimes between evil and evil. Political reason is a
> computing principle. (Quoted in Paine, *Common Sense*,
> p. 101)

The metaphor is apt. The politics of social fragmentation is based for Madison on the most fundamental natural division in the faculties of men: unequal faculties of acquiring property. Madison says:

> From the protection of different and unequal faculties of
> acquiring property [the first object of government] the
> possession of different degrees and kinds of property
> immediately results; and from the influence of these on
> the sentiments and views of the respective proprietors
> ensues a division of the society. (*Federalist Papers*,
> p. 78)

Justice is for Madison the balance between the parts of the fragmented society, and his examples make it clear that the most significant separation which must be balanced is that between creditors and debtors:

> Is a law proposed concerning private debt? It is a
> question to which the creditors are parties on one side
> and the debtors on the other. Justice ought to hold the
> balance between them. (*Federalist Papers*, pp. 79-80)

Combination of the majority in society makes this conception of justice impossible. Fortunately for Madison, he envisioned a social fragmentation and geographical dispersions so systematic that combination would be difficult to achieve. Thus he argued that a "common motive" to invade the rights of the "minority" would not culminate in action because it will be "difficult for all who feel it to discover their own strength and to act in unison with each other" (p. 83). The only specific examples Madison gives of what united and unjust action would look like are the following:

A rage for paper money, for an abolition of debts, for an equal division of property. (p. 84)

The core of these examples is the abolition of debt: justice lies between credit and debt. Debtors who would abolish the distinction which justice must enforce are attacking that which is natural, the principle of societal order as indebtedness. Indebtedness is the concrete experience of social life which must be preserved for justice to be possible, for the social diseases of instability to be prevented. Whatever attacks this principle is, in terms of Burke's definition of political reason, "unreasonable," since it attacks the framework within which "computation" has meaning. The abolition of indebtedness is the substance of injustice.

The assumption of social fragmentation, the idea that it is separation that holds society together, is one of the persistent paradoxes of modern political theory which is inexplicable apart from an understanding of the logic of indebtedness which gives it meaning. The absolutistic character of this assumption—that those who do not hold to the respect for separation are unreasonable and perverse—suggests that deviations from this common standard of justice, since they are viewed as irrational, inspire irrational fright. (Compare Hartz, *Liberal Tradition*, p. 53.) The sense of a society which is held together by fragmentation is thus both powerfully individualistic and profoundly totalitarian, and poses the paradox which Tocqueville first noted in America, that "individualism" and "conformity" are two sides of the same problem, the problem of public opinion. Put another way: Adams's picture of American other-directedness is perfectly compatible with the logic of social fragmentation: the ever-present terror of public esteem is, in this sense, a substitute for the absence of concrete societal integration, an abstraction superimposed over powerlessness and indebtedness. It is to the nature of this abstraction and to the essentially compensatory responses of the American Transcendentalists that we now must turn.

The Powerful Stranger

The limits of the possessive unconscious are revealed as fundamentally compensatory wherever futility, impotence, and estrangement become values in themselves and are thus transformed into a peculiar sort of strength. And this strength which rationalizes the absence of efficacy, which resigns the actor to a solipsistic universe where power is either his own inner possession or abstract and other than himself, was clearly expressed by Emerson:

> ... self-reliance is precisely that secret,—to make your
> supposed deficiency redundancy. If I am true, the theory
> is, the very want of action, my very impotency, shall
> become a greater excellency than all skill and toil.
> (*Emerson Selections*, p. 146)

The transformation of deficiency into redundancy is the substance of the logic of compensation. That the self can be true not in spite of but because of its "impotency," because of its inability to act, because of its lack of connection with a contingent reality—this is the message of the tradition of authentic self-possession. There is, in other words, a dichotomy—I have termed it above "the logic of abstraction"—which concerns the estrangement of power and which is present wherever the ownership metaphor is applied to human identity: as power becomes more withdrawn and abstractly associated with an externality defined as a "medley of other things," where the self is such that it can be at-a-loss (nowhere, in *extasis*), power within powerlessness entails taking this abstractness upon the self.

This process was, I think accurately, described by Tocqueville when he noted that in what he called a community "without public virtue," where things happen without the individual's knowledge or concurrence, such an individual would come to see public questions as "unconnected with himself and as the property of a powerful stranger whom he calls the government" (*Democracy*, Vol. 1, p. 96). Tocqueville's work is an attempt to follow this out: how in the face of this "powerful stranger" people come to be powerful strangers unto one another, their power presuming estrangement, structured out of their impotence, abstract because it is the negation of an abstraction, because it chooses the logic of abstraction as its own.

Tocqueville's analysis suggests that for modernity, equality of condition refers to the experience of being equally powerless, equally separate from others. Cut off from traditional bonds, people come to be thrown back upon themselves and, in the face of the powerful stranger, the absence of a concrete public connection with others (contingency or mediation) entails the taking of the whole of an abstract "mankind" into the self. The isolated individual, self-possessed and self-contained, relates to himself and to mankind simultaneously and without mediation. Tocqueville makes this point in a discussion of the sources of poetry in America when he argues,

> The general similitude of individuals, which renders any
> one of them taken separately an improper subject of
> poetry, allows poets to include them all in the same
> imagery. (Vol. 1, p. 96)

The explanation is that "faith in intermediate agents" is overcast, and there is, for example, no mediation between "citizen and nation," individual and mankind (Vol. 2, p. 78).

But the absence of mediation puts us squarely within the logic of compensation, beyond the experience of being indebted to others, but limited by the need to be indebted to oneself alone. Thus limited, individuals

> . . . owe nothing to any man . . . expect nothing from any
> man; they acquire the habit of always considering
> themselves as standing alone, and they are apt to
> imagine that their whole destiny is in their hands. (Vol.
> 2, p. 78)

Such a situation, Tocqueville argues, separates the individual from his contemporaries, "throws him back forever upon himself alone and threatens in the end to confine him entirely within the solitude of his own heart" (Vol. 2, pp. 104-105).

The question which Tocqueville poses is therefore: Given the modern tendency toward estrangement and separation, how would people come to give meaning and coherence to their actions? Emerson provides an answer to this question, which still haunts our social unconscious. Emerson says: yes, the world is everywhere in fragments; but this is only an illusory problem, only one of society's tricks which seduce men into thinking that union is a political problem, and that therefore it might be a political construct. The true problem, Emerson argued, lies elsewhere. Or, as he says,

> The reason why the world lacks unity, and lies broken
> and in heaps, is because man is disunited with himself.
> (*Emerson Selections*, p. 145)

Thus Emerson formulates the problem in terms of alienation from self, being out of touch with, not being true to oneself. Where Tocqueville suggests that the fascination with problems of the self is related to the more primary context of modern civilization, Emerson deemphasizes a political response to the problem. Social action was, for Emerson, one of the conditioned and contingent human states which must be transcended in favor of the "unconditional abstractness of the self which creates its world instead of acting in it" (Anderson, *Imperial*, p. 44).

This perception was evident in Emerson's response to the project of Brook Farm. In 1840, when friends asked Emerson to join in the creation of an experimental utopian community, they argued that he would in joining them be able to live according to his own theories. He responded by telling them that they had misunderstood the thrust of his theories, and that therefore they had mistaken what evidence would pass for their proof. He wrote in his journal at the time:

> I do not wish to remove from my present prison to a
> prison a little larger. I wish to break all prisons. I have
> not yet conquered my own house. It irks and repents
> me. Shall I raise the siege of this hencoop, and march
> baffled away to a pretended siege of Babylon? It seems
> to me that so to do were to dodge the problem I am set
> to solve, and to hide my impotency in the thick of the
> crowd . . . to join this body would be to traverse all my
> long trumpeted theory, and the instinct which spoke
> from it, that one man is a counterpoise to a city, that his
> solitude is more prevalent and beneficial than the
> concert of crowds. (*Emerson Selections*, p. 145)

If I am true, the theory is. The theory, the philosophical extension of the logic of the possessive unconscious, was, of course, what Emerson called "self-reliance." It is epitomized in the motto which he chose to introduce his essay of that title: "Do not seek yourself outside yourself." In this idea Emerson expressed the limits of the dichotomy of indebtedness:

... now we are a mob. Man does not stand in awe of
man, nor is his genius admonished to stay at home, to
put itself in communication with the internal ocean, but
it goes abroad to beg a cup of water of the urns of other
men. (p. 159)

Indebted to others, beggars at the urns of others, individuals come
to experience society as an autonomous force above them, depriv-
ing them of choice:

... most natures are insolvent, and cannot satisfy their
own wants ... we have not chosen, society has chosen
for us. (p. 161)

The attribution of agency to the autonomous and abstract force
of "society" meant for Emerson that social activities were necessarily limited to those which were directionless and compromis-
ing:

... there is a spirit of cowardly compromise and seeming
which intimates ... a life without love, an activity
without aim. (p. 202)

Here we have Emerson's formulation of the problem of aim inhibition, the separation of aim and activity which is at the heart of
Hobbesian institutions, of mechanisms which enforce reliance on
things outside the self (such as law, the marketplace, the regu-
larity and regulation of property relations). Property, above all else
for Emerson, symbolizes this principle of external reliance in that
the estimation of the worth of a man through what he has, the
Hobbesian principle that the worth of a man is his price, has, so
Emerson argues, warped and contorted the nature of man.

... the reliance on property, including reliance on
governments which protect it, is the want of
self-reliance. Men have looked away from themselves
and at things so long that they have come to esteem ...
institutions as guards of property.... They measure their
esteem of each other by what each has, not by what each
is. (p. 167)

But all relationships are property relationships: what is
problematic about the reliance on property is its externality. So
long as men rely on a principle outside of themselves, their aim—

the search for independence—will be inhibited; so long as property is outside the self, men are dependent upon society for the validation of their worth. Thus Emerson's response to the problem of social indebtedness is not an attack on the logic of indebtedness itself, but rather a plea for a more sophisticated form of property, a plea for man as his own property.

> . . . that which a man is . . . is living property, which
> does not wait for the beck of rulers, or mobs, or
> revolutions, or fire, or storm or bankruptcies, but
> perpetually renews itself. (p. 167)

Having equated the logic of external relationships of indebtedness with all possible forms of societal mediation, having defined contingency and any relational identity as dependence upon externalities, Emerson argues that the human spirit will be perpetually disappointed if it expects fulfillment in social or political activity:

> A political victory, a rise of rents, the recovery of your
> sick or the return of your absent friend, or some other
> favorable event raises your spirits, and you think good
> days are preparing for you. Do not believe it. Nothing
> can bring you peace but yourself. (p. 168)

To care about any project in the world, to engage in work toward a common goal, is for Emerson to desert oneself. Work in this sense entails dependence upon others, and is equated with action by Emerson. Since work demands that the self perish, Emerson simply says: "If I cannot work, at least I need not lie" (p. 203). There is in this perspective what Emerson calls a "double consciousness": one part conscious of the limits of work, that "it really signifies little what we do," the other conscious of the infinite possibilities of the self. It is Emerson's burden to argue that self and work are irreconcilable, that one's work in the broad sense of one's social possibilities must be transcended. What this means is that a man must not commit himself to public action. Once commitment occurs the self becomes a "committed person," interpreted and judged by others, "watched by the sympathy or the hatred of hundreds, whose affections must now enter into his account." He concludes:

Who can thus avoid all pledges and, having observed,

observe again from the same unaffected, unbiased, unbribable, unaffrighted innocence,—must always be formidable. (p. 149)

As Hobbes's concern was the creation of a man capable of keeping promises, a "dependable" or reliable man, and as this dependability has come to symbolize external indebtedness for Emerson, avoidance of reliability must be necessary for self-reliance to be possible. Emerson transforms what Tocqueville saw as the separation of men cut off from one another, as their loneliness deprived of public connection, as their powerlessness and inability to act meaningfully in concert with others, into a conception of strength. He provides a glimpse into the psychology of political indifference: that out of despair over powerlessness, men might come to value impotence above all else, if only because it is the one thing they can be sure of.

Certain only of powerlessness, experiencing power as abstract and anonymous dominance, dominance by society's "conspiracy against the manhood of everyone of its members" (*Emerson Selections*, p. 149), the individual who would be autonomous must struggle against a society which is, for Emerson, a "joint stock company." Such a society, Emerson thought, demanded that the experience of contingency was necessarily the experience of the market place where fragments of humanity were bought and sold. To be dependent on society meant in effect that the self would be parceled out and put up for sale. The buying and selling of selves was most pronounced in the "divided or social state" where power had been so "minutely subdivided and peddled out" that members of society "have suffered amputation from the trunk, and strut about so many walking monsters,—a good finger, a neck, a stomach, an elbow, but never a man" (*Emerson Selections*, p. 64).

This description parallels Nietzsche's remarks on the "fragments of the future." Both Nietzsche and Emerson mount an attack on what Nietzsche called the "flies" of the marketplace, the buzz of commercial civilization which fragmented men on demand. But for Nietzsche, this was a critique of a particular historical development; for Emerson it formed the basis of a critique of society in general. From a description of the solipsistic psychology of commercial society—"Is it not pathetic that the action of men on men is so partial?"—Emerson moves to an ontological statement about man's nature: ". . . man is insular and cannot be touched. Every man is an infinitely repellent orb, and holds his individual being on that condition" (*Emerson Selections*, p. 61).

To define the nature of man as infinitely repellent is to say that no meaningful connection, no essential "touching" is possible between men; all that can be between men becomes subsumed within men: community becomes communion with oneself, mediation becomes an *intra* personal phenomenon. Emerson becomes, in other words, a communist internally, a communist of the self. Thus in speaking of the utopian socialists of his day, of Ripley and Owen, he says:

> My doing my office entitles me to your doing yours. This is the secret after which the Communists are coarsely and externally striving. (p. 283)

You do your thing, and I'll do mine: respect for the partial and fragmented "offices" of men entails from this perspective a transcendence of all relationships with others, of the "medley of other things." Relationships are, again, necessarily those of indebtedness, and the perpetual problem of those who are indebted, the calculation of their "accounts," their ability to repay their debts and secure repayment in turn—the infinite burden of the behavioral self—this is what Emerson attempts to avoid.

It is in this sense that the logic of indebtedness is at the core of what Emerson termed "the circular or compensatory character of every human action" (p. 168). Emerson's philosophy is a philosophy of compensation which begins with the assumption that

> . . . nothing can be given; everything is sold; love compels love; hatred, hatred; action and reaction are always equal . . . (p. 99)

and culminates in the principle which Emerson attributes to St. Bernard, "Nobody can harm me but myself" (p. 15). I have met the enemy and he is me.

This principle is a final rendering of the logic of possession, and it collapses any tension between action and reaction totally within the self. Its corollary is, of course, that no one can help me but myself, that I owe it to myself alone to structure that psychological space between giving and selling, recognizing that nothing can be given *because* everything is sold, that selling equals relating to others and that the need of relationship must itself therefore be transcended. Emerson speaks of the "self-helping man":

> Welcome evermore to Gods and men is the self-helping
> man. For him all doors are flung wide, . . . all eyes
> follow him with desire. Our love goes out to him
> because he did not need it. (p. 163)

The formation of this psychological space between giving and selling, the refuge that is self-possession, is the constitutive element of what I have called the schizophrenic vision.

Where all relationships are experienced as property relations, where repayment is impossible because indebtedness is inevitable, then taking this guilt upon the self, choosing it as one's ownmost relationship to oneself, becomes the best, the most "authentic" way of living not a slave because not a master. Self-possession is, in other words, the last defense against others; the schizophrenic vision is the last, the most pervasive, and the best compensation of the behavioral self.

Emerson expressed the idea of the schizophrenic vision most directly in what he referred to as the *experience* of "double consciousness." Men experience two forms of consciousness, Emerson argued: one ("the understanding") was rooted in day-to-day activities of fragmentation and indebtedness, and was the consciousness of imperfection and division; the other (the "soul") was rooted in the "private experience" of infinitude and perfection. Emerson put it this way:

> The worst feature of this double consciousness is that
> the two lives of the understanding and of the soul, which
> we lead, really show very little relation to each other;
> one prevails now, all buzz and din; and the other
> prevails then, all infinitude and paradise; and, with the
> progress of life, the two discover no greater disposition
> to reconcile themselves. (p. 204)

But Emerson, of course, proposed a method of reconciliation. He expressed it best in the concluding passages of his essay on *Nature*:

> Build therefore your own world. As fast as you conform
> your life to the pure idea in your mind, that will unfold
> its great proportions. A correspondent revolution in
> things will attend the influx of the spirit. So fast will
> disagreeable appearances, swine, spiders, pests,
> mad-houses, prisons, enemies, vanish; they are
> *temporary* and shall be seen no more. (p. 56; my
> emphasis)

This perspectival change, the ability to transform the world by transcending its *temporality* and finitude, is well illustrated by Emerson, and following him, by Thoreau, in the Transcendentalist conception of friendship. Since it is indicative of the logic of the schizophrenic vision, we will turn to it here.

Emerson remarks in his journals that he has often had "fine fancies about a person" which gave him "delicious hours," but that these fancies were without issue. The joy of fancy "yields no fruit," the presence of the person disappoints. What disappoints most is the expectation of reciprocity in a relationship.

> It has seemed to me lately more possible than I knew, to
> carry a friendship greatly, on one side, without due
> correspondence to the other. Why should I cumber
> myself with regrets that the receiver is not capacious?
> . . . It is thought a disgrace to love unrequited. But the
> great will see that true love cannot be unrequited. True
> love transcends the unworthy object and dwells and
> broods on the eternal, and when the poor interposed
> mask crumbles, it is not sad, but feels rid of so much
> earth and feels its independence the surer. Yet these
> things may hardly be said without a sort of treachery to
> the relation. The essence of friendship is entireness, a
> total magnanimity and trust. It must not surmise or
> provide for infirmity. It treats its object as a god, that it
> may deify both. (*Emerson Selections*, pp. 133-134)

True love *cannot* be unrequited: it is not connected with or dependent upon the unworthy object, which is part of the world of disagreeable appearances, masks which only crumble and upon which one cannot depend. It is beyond contingency and temporality, for there it would "live outside itself," in connectedness with another.

It is in this sense that, for Thoreau as well, one finds in the friend the infinite and the universal: one becomes persuaded of the richness of humanity, absorbed by the drama of that which is infinitely pure and good, immortal and holy, in contrast to the finite, profane, and unworthy. Friendship, for Thoreau, is "a drama in which the parties have no part to act" (*Walden*, p. 478). The friend is not cherished in his concrete presence, but for what is expressed through him.

I love thee not as something private and personal which

is *your own*, but as something universal and worthy of love, *which I have found.* (p. 478)

That is, I love you as something that is *mine*, as my ideal. Thus while there is respect at the core of Thoreau's conception of friendship, it is not respect for another; rather:

> This is what I would like . . . respecting you as I respect my ideal. Never to profane one another by word or action, even by a thought. Between us, if necessary, let there be no acquaintance. (p. 478)

Beyond word and deed, the strongest experiences of friendship are not located in present interaction with others, but in reminiscence of the past or anticipation of the future; friends experience this paradox:

> When they say farewell, then indeed we begin to keep them company. How often we find ourselves turning our backs on our actual friends, that we may go and meet their ideal cousins. (p. 375)

Similarly, friendship "exists at all only by condescension and anticipation of the remotest future" (p. 383). The qualities of a friend become more noble; in other words, at a distance.

> I always assign to him a nobler employment in my absence than I ever find him engaged in. (p. 380)

Thus the imperfections, the finitude, and the limitations of contingency are modified and transcended in true friendship.

> All the abuses which are the object of reform with the philanthropist, the statesman, and the housekeeper, are unconsciously amended in the intercourse of friends. (p. 376)

This is the amendment of the possessive unconscious. Commitment to one's friend in the enterprises in which he is engaged, in the world of his abuses, and his projects to affect those abuses, which his concrete presence represents, is, in short, inauthentic.

Our actual friends are but distant relations to those to

whom we are pledged. We never exchange more than
three words with a Friend in our lives on that level to
which our thoughts and feelings almost habitually rise.
One goes forth prepared to say "Sweet Friends!" and the
salutation is "Damn your eyes." (p. 375)

Damn your eyes for making me be seen, for reducing me to the
level of temporality and contingency, for being-here rather than
absent, for possessing me, for making me a part of your world, for
threatening to engage me in the redress of your abuses, for taking
away my soul. Here Thoreau expresses the absolute rejection of
Adams's principle of *spectemur agendo*, let us be watched in the
doing. To be watched in the doing is to perform, to do for others,
and the performative identity is dependent upon the evaluation of
others.

I value and trust those who love and praise my
aspiration rather than my performance. If you would not
stop to look at me, but look whither I am looking and
further, then my education could not dispense with your
company. (p. 386)

The classical idea of performance (the root of the word is *four-
nir*, to furnish, accomplish, complete) is that an act is incomplete
unless others see it, and Adams tried to invoke this as the sense of
spectemur agendo. Yet performance for Thoreau means not the
enrichment of one's acts, but the loss of one's self, a form of self-
abuse. The only sense of completion about an act that matters is a
completion which avoids being defined by or connected with others, an experience of integration which is compatible with the essential separation and distance which must be preserved between
men.

It is Whitman, I think, who best formulates this remarkable integration principle of modernity, the principle of the powerful
stranger who ties his world together in that

. . . compact, well-join'd scheme, myself disintegrated,
every one disintegrated yet part of the scheme. (*Leaves
of Grass*, p. 134, "Crossing Brooklyn Ferry")

This overall scheme was for Whitman expressed through the
metaphor of the open road which offered a perpetual process of

separation and dissociation, a vision of the destiny of the self defined beyond connectedness with others.

> You but arrive at the city to which you were destin'd,
> You hardly settle/yourself to satisfaction before you are
> call'd by an irresistible call to depart,/ you shall be
> treated to the ironical smiles and mockings of those who
> remain behind you,/ What beckonings of love you
> receive you shall only answer with passionate kisses of
> parting,/ You shall not allow the holds of those who
> spread their reach'd hands toward you. (p. 130, "Song of
> the Open Road")

For the wandering stranger the journey along the open road is, as
Whitman says, endless as it is beginningless, a perpetual search
beyond the outstretched hands, the grasping indebtedness of society: freedom is always away from connectedness with others. The
substance of this freedom is what Whitman called "completeness in
separation":

> Underneath the fluctuations of the expressions of society
> . . . we see steadily pressing ahead and strengthening
> itself, even in the midst of immense tendencies toward
> aggregation, this image of completeness in separation, of
> individual personal dignity, of a single person . . .
> characterized in the main not from extrinsic
> acquirements or position, but in the pride of himself or
> herself alone; and as an eventual conclusion and
> summing up (or else the entire scheme of things is
> aimless, a cheat, a crash), the simple idea that the last,
> best dependence is to be upon humanity itself. (p. 499,
> "Democratic Vistas")

The last, best defense against connectedness is the paradox that
one can be complete *within* separation, that the isolate individual,
complete within himself, is the highest expression of humanity.
Dependence on humanity, like Hobbes's conception of dependence on the Sovereign, like Rousseau's notion of dependence on
things, not on men, is dependence upon an abstraction. As
Tocqueville understood, the sources of poetry in America revolve
around the images of abstract unification (humanity, mankind) as a
direct extension of the experience of the isolated individual, not
around the mediation or connectedness of social interaction. But
completeness can be achieved amidst separation only by virtue of

becoming beyond the need of others, beyond connectedness and relationship; it can be achieved only *immediately*:

> Henceforth I whimper no more, postpone no more, need nothing . . . strong and content I travel the open road. (p. 124, "Song of the Open Road")

A vision of gratification beyond need, Whitman's view searches for a way to talk about unity in the context of inevitable estrangement. So long as men meet only as strangers, they pass each other by, self-possessed and confirmed in their mutual anonymity. Here nothing can be lost because there is nothing left to lose. As in "The Ballad of Bobbie McGee," this is Whitman's conception of freedom, just another word for nothing left to lose:

> Passing stranger! . . .
> I am not to speak to you, I am to think of you
> when I sit alone or wake
> at night alone,
> I am to wait, I do not doubt I am to meet you again,
> I am to see to it that I do not lose you. (p. 108, "To a Stranger")

Thus, in Whitman, the psychology of the possessive unconscious achieves mythic and paradoxical proportions. As D. H. Lawrence said about Fenimore Cooper, "true myth concerns itself centrally with the onward adventure of the integral soul," with the "isolate, almost selfless, stoic, enduring man." And this, Lawrence added, is "the very intrinsic-most American" (*Classic American*, pp. 62-63).

Where we see these mythic aspects in their extreme in Whitman, we find that beneath the psychology of possession, guilt, and indebtedness there lies a metaphoric association between the selfless, isolate wanderer and his identity as what I would call a "prodigal giver." We have seen this sense of giving implicit in a variety of perspectives: whether it is understood as expressing the freedom of one who is not indebted to others or that of one who so completely and authentically possesses his world that there is nothing in his experience which (as Merleau-Ponty expressed it) he has not "put there," the idea of the prodigal giver is an image of total self-containment and the impossibility of receiving anything essential from others. From this perspective, the situation of the receiver comes to represent that experience of inauthentic indebtedness, the root of Hobbes's conception of the desperate debtor and the anxiety that gratitude is a form of retribution. Thus it is the case, I think, that as N. O. Brown says,

> The modern psychology of possession is superimposed over a deeper psychology of giving. (*Life*, p. 264)

To explore this depth-psychological level is to confront our most basic assumptions about the nature of civilization. To understand the psychology of giving is to face the most primal myths which underlie the politics of the behavioral self. Before turning systematically to the relationship between giving and possession, I wish to conclude this chapter with a discussion of the myth of the prodigal giver in America.

The Prodigal Giver: Mythic Desocialization

Speaking of the second generation American Puritan, Perry Miller argued that his greatest problem, one which has preoccupied Americans ever since, was the problem of identity. For the American, no longer sure for what or for whom he was working, knowing only that he is going somewhere, no longer Pilgrim but rather a wanderer, his search for identity, Miller maintained, could take place nowhere but within himself (*Errand*, p. 15). This theme, that one must wander in search of self, has become a modern litany: one which, from Whitman through Kerouac, is our most pervasive expression of the mythic desocialization of our lives. The hero of this myth is the prodigal giver.

In contemporary culture, whether the mythic hero is a fugitive or one who must run for his life, whether the scene is the gangland 30s or the American West, the theme is the same: wander in search of self, escape from connectedness, reject relatedness to others, but give of yourself prodigally. Here I will present just one example of the myth from the mass media, followed by a brief analysis of its meaning. "The Man Called Shenandoah" was an evening television series shown in prime time several years ago. Although it no longer exists, its format will be familiar.

The tragic hero of the series was merely "called" Shenandoah, known to others only by this name. He had no other identity. An amnesia sufferer (typical of the media presentation), he was doomed, as the commentary went, to wander: "following trails that lead to dead ends," to nowhere. He moved from town to town, hoping, yet fearing, that someone would recognize him, that is to say, would help him recollect the self he had lost. In this endeavor he was constantly frustrated, yet, as he said, "a man has to live." Thus he wandered, away from that place where he belonged, cursed by the fact that he was nonetheless dependent upon others for affirmation of self.

Amnesia is a symbolically apt term by which to describe the loss of a fixed point of reference (connectedness), the absence of the memory of continuity and identity. But Shenandoah is not merely separated from himself, but from others as well, for he is a forgotten man in a dual sense. Not only is he aware of not being his true self, but he has lost the ability to recognize those who could in turn affirm his identity: he is in *extasis*, for he must possess himself or be possessed. He can in no way accept identification by others, and hence must be suspicious of any proffered affirmation. Yet, wherever Shenandoah wanders, he behaves as if he were related: he does "good" deeds without being a part of the shared community of values within which such an ethical adjective has meaning. Thus he gives of himself to others, and magically the initial rejection which he received as a stranger in town turns to affection: he is asked to stay, to belong to the community. Yet he rejects this offer, and wanders on his way.

The most important aspect of this myth is that the act of rejection of connectedness is always viewed as a free choice. Yet choice here is intimately tied to rationalization. The myth presents an absurd sense of responsibility to others. Without any need of affirmation, without any sense of belonging to a community of shared norms, the hero is obliged to give to those from whom affirmation was either suspect or not desired. To Shenandoah, like Whitman's stranger, this affirmation was always offered. That is, the powerful stranger imagines himself surrounded by a world that is in need, which needs him, though he does not need it. All are indebted to Shenandoah; he is their redemption though he exists only on the periphery of their lives and is indebted only to himself. He rejects connectedness because it entails indebtedness, he *chooses* to wander, values his autonomy, and finds in social relationships only imperfection, dependence, and unfreedom. His freedom is possible only as a stranger.

The powerful stranger has, in other words, chosen estrangement as a way of life, chosen disintegration and separation from others. Not merely does the wanderer consent to suffer estrangement from his fellows, but rather he actually affirms this state out of fear that it might be chosen for him. These lines of W. H. Auden are expressive of this phenomenon of mythic desocialization:

> What fear of freedom then
> Causes our clasping hands
> To make in miniature
> That earth anew, and now
> By choice instead of chance
> To suffer from the same
> Attraction and untruth
> Suspicion and respect? (*Anxiety*, p. 73)

Attraction and suspicion are inseparable from the point of view of the wanderer: those who offer acceptance and affirmation of identity are necessarily suspected of treachery since they provide the ever-present threat of dependence and absorption into the anonymity of the they. Untruth and respect are similarly inseparable: respect for self (from *respicere*, to look back at) obtains only a picture of the untruth of the wandering identity. Where the essential limitations of the logic of indebtedness are presented as unalterable, estranged relationships are the normal conditions out of which the myth is constructed. To be able to endure estrangement, the man who must continue to live must internalize the very conditions which cause his suffering: hence he defines his identity in terms of the rejection of contingency, and chooses to remain estranged. Thus by choice instead of chance the world is rationalized—made anew and in miniature through identification with the wandering ideal, the best possible artifact that can be created by hands that are clasped in behavioral despair.

The point to be stressed is that suffering, estrangement, and indebtedness become more understandable when they are chosen *as one's own* even though this choice may be nothing more than a rationalization. Telling the myth of the individual who is so strong within himself that he can reject gratuitous offers of friendship conveys implicitly the undercurrent fear that friendship may not in fact be offered at all. The individual responds to this feeling of insecurity and threat of dependence upon others by asserting that he is completely secure within himself; his stance is essentially passive. It is in this sense that self-creativity and self-definition ultimately become self-delusion, an escape from the fear that one may not meaningfully belong in any other way.

All are indebted to the prodigal giver, because he refuses to receive. All love goes out to him, as Emerson said, because he does not need it. Thus the logical conclusion, the mythic symbol of redemption of the anxieties of the desperate debtor, is the figure of the prodigal giver, the heroic rendition of the situation of the powerful stranger. This logical result of the estrangement of power, this vision of an individual who is a community unto himself, totally self-possessed, represents the most complete desocialization of identity, the final development of self-fetishism. It is in Nietzsche's *Zarathustra* that the political psychology of the prodigal giver is most completely articulate. There is a pathos about the Nietzschean rendition of prodigality which captures the peculiar tension which has been the inspiration of these essays: that freedom is idiocy.

I want to turn to this pathos explicitly.

6
The Political Psychology
of Permission

*The time has gone when mere accidents could still
happen to me; and what could still come to me now
that was not mine already? What returns, what
finally comes home to me, is my own self and what
of myself has long been in strange lands and
scattered among all things and accidents.*
(Nietzsche, *Zarathustra*, p. 264)

An introductory text on abnormal psychology describes what it
calls a recent neurotic disorder in the West, "existential neurosis":

> The cognitive component of the existential neurosis is
> meaningless, or chronic inability to believe in the truth,
> importance, usefulness, or interest value of any of the
> things one is engaged in. . . . The most characteristic
> [emotional] features . . . are blandness and boredom,
> punctuated by periods of depression . . . but more
> important is the introspective and objectively observable
> fact that activities are not chosen. (Davidson and Neale,
> *Abnormal Psychology*, p. 148)

"Existential neurosis" is the experience of life as an accident,
not chosen by the individual. In order to have a more healthy personal development, the text suggests that existential neurotics attempt to "have an active internal life, which they maintain whatever happens in the external world" (p. 150).

Expressing this attempt in a recently popular song, Olivia
Newton-John asks: "Have you never tried to find the comfort from
inside you?" The therapeutic of the comfort from inside is the last
consolation of the disintegration of modern Western society.
Freud once commented about one of his patients that though the

man showed some signs of paranoia, his recovery from illness was virtually complete, in that he had "felt normal and behaved unexceptionally, in spite of the war having robbed him of his home, possessions and family relationships" (Freud, *Therapy*, p. 235). This is the consolation of idiocy, one of the most current expressions of our *extasis*.

Writing in his notebooks about his "innovations," Nietzsche listed: ". . . intellectual pessimism; critique of morality, disintegration of the last consolation" (*Power*, #417). He then outlined the development of his thinking:

> (1) My endeavor to oppose decay and increasing weakness of personality. I sought a new *center*.
> (2) Impossibility of this endeavor recognized.
> (3) Thereupon I advanced further down the road of disintegration—where I found new sources of strength for individuals . . . I perceived that the state of disintegration, in which individual natures can perfect themselves as never before—is an image and isolated example of existence in general. (*Power*, #417)

The perfection of individuals in a context of disintegration: this might as well characterize the project of modern Western political culture as the development of Nietzsche's thinking. The more thorough the disintegration of modern society, the more perfect the nature of the individual.

The comfort within oneself proceeds in direct proportion to this disintegration. To destroy the last consolation: this is the hardness of Nietzsche, his refusal to waffle in the face of what he knew. What he knew was that the supramoral, autonomous self, puffed up in its new self-love and filled with meaning, was an *example* of societal disintegration.

If we desire to know deeply and with understanding, Nietzsche said, there is a drop of cruelty turned against oneself. Push through to a new center, the autonomous individual, but remember that this proud creation of human art is carved out of a context of social disintegration and decay. Perhaps he learned it from the best part of Rousseau, who wrote about modern life as the progressive development of the individual and the progressive decrepitude of the species.

In this context, the virtues which Nietzsche extols are dangerous, idiotic, and finally catastrophic. The freedom he envisioned is a description of our world. Here I will relate the central aspects of this vision, so that we may better see ourselves and what we have become.

The Politics of Virtue

There is in Nietzsche a political psychology of freedom which he called the "politics of virtue." This psychology was rooted in his understanding of the human dialectic between power and fear.

Nietzsche thought that fear was the mother of morals. He described the modern experience of the fear that nourishes morality in this passage:

> . . . domination, sensitivity to pain, restlessness, haste, and hustling grow continually . . . it becomes easier and easier to recognize this whole commotion, this so-called "civilization," and . . . the individual, faced with this tremendous machinery, loses courage and submits. (*Power*, #33)

For Nietzsche it was the nation state and the marketplace which are the contexts that organize and give meaning to the disintegration and distraction of the modern world.

But from within the bowels of the nation state and admidst the chaos and disintegration of the marketplace, Nietzsche projected a vision beyond the state and the marketplace, conceived a center of solitude from which to clear away the noise and distraction:

> Flee, my friend, into your solitude! I see you dazed by the noise of the great men and stung all over by the stings of the little men. . . . Where solitude ceases the marketplace begins. (*Zarathustra*, p. 163)

The great men who lead the state, which Nietzsche called the "New Idol" and the superfluous men, filled with gall and self-disgust, live what Nietzsche thought was "the slow suicide of all" called "life" (p. 163). In this thought is the basic understanding of the literature of authenticity in its critique of the idolatry of everyday life.

For Nietzsche the roots of this critique began, as did Marx's, with a critique of religion. Like Marx, Nietzsche understood religion to be a projection of the oppressed and the downtrodden, an expression of the "sublime self-deception that interprets weakness as freedom" (Nietzsche, *Morals*, p. 46). "Fear and terror" at one's *own* "feeling of power" is at the root of this projection, where personal power is displaced onto a "stronger person, a divinity," or a drug which accounts for the feeling.

As Nietzsche understands us, we are generally afraid of our own powers and abilities. But if fear is the mother of morals, what is the root of our fear?

Akin with the etymological root of *fear* are the Old English *faer* (which meant sudden calamity, danger), the Old Saxon *var* (meaning ambush), and the Old High German *fara* (meaning ambush, stratagem, danger, and deceit).

The danger of deceitful ambush, of being carried away or seized is most clear in the etymological root of *deception* (from *de* + *capere*, to take away, seize, lead into error). The experience of deception, lying, being led astray is at the root of our fear. Self-deception is the last consolation of our fears; self-indulgence is our greatest error.

Error is a *condition*, as we still express in the phrase "you are in error." To be in error is to wander, etymologically (error from *errare*, to wander): the wanderers are in error.

But Nietzsche was a wanderer, and his most integrative work, *Thus Spake Zarathustra*, is the expression of the Dionysian truths of wandering. Received customary wisdom teaches that to wander is to err. Nietzsche taught that this teaching is a deception. The wanderer learns that "the character of existence is not 'true,' is *false"(Power*, #12). Against the falsity of this fearful existence Nietzsche taught a Dionysian politics, which he called *virtue:* the virtue of the Renaissance, "*virtu*, moraline-free virtue" (#317).

This virtue, Nietzsche said, is "unprofitable, imprudent, it isolates . . . it rouses enmity toward order, toward the lies that are concealed in every order, institution, actuality" (#317). The politics of Dionysian virtue "does precisely all that is generally forbidden"; it is recognized as virtue because it does not desire to be recognized, it does not presuppose virtue everywhere, it does not suffer from the absence of virtue "but on the contrary regards this as the distancing relationship on the basis of which there is something to honor in virtue." Virtue does not propagandize, "It permits no one to judge it, because it is virtue for itself" (#317). The absence of virtue everywhere, the disintegration of modern life, is to be regarded as the basis for virtue as a "distancing relationship." If people are increasingly distanced from one another, then this distance will be the root of their virtue.

Nietzschian virtue permits no one to judge it: its Dionysian standards are for itself. Virtue in this sense is located not as a characteristic of relationships between people, but as an attribute of one's relationship to oneself. It permits no judgment external to its values: judgment is a relationship with oneself.

The man of virtue (*virtu*) is a man (*vir*) in the sense of a "virtuoso." Such a man is not a "virtuous" (in the sense of "good") man for Nietzsche. The "good" man is simply "conforming to a pattern of man that is fixed once and for all" (*Zarathustra*, p. 174).

But genuine, Dionysian virtue is no longer believed in; Nietzsche wrote:

> . . . to restore it, someone would have to know how to take it to market as an unfamiliar form of adventure and excess. (*Power*, #323)

If Nietzsche could see our world he would marvel at the ingenuity with which virtue has made its appearance in the marketplace. When virtue goes to market it becomes authenticity.

The basis for the accommodation of virtue to the marketplace is present in Nietzsche's thought. For Nietzsche, genuine virtues are produced from "out of oneself . . . as one's most personal self-defence and necessity, as conditions of precisely *our own* existence and growth, which we recognize and acknowledge independently of whether other men grow with us under similar or different conditions" (#326).

This is an idiotic virtue: the assumption that what I am can "grow" independently of other people. The new courage which Nietzsche taught was a courage beyond *a priori* truths. He thought that the means toward increased responsibility, self-assurance, and the ability to posit goals for oneself were "isolation through interests in prescription that are the reverse of those which are average today; habituation to reverse evaluations; distance as a pathos; a free conscience in those things that today are most individual and prohibited" (#898). To grow against the grain was the advantage which Nietzsche sought, the advance of "detachment from one's age" (#859).

But this detachment is *extasis* raised to its highest idiocy. Isolation and distance are the day-to-day virtues of idiot man, that man who can transform his distance from others into a virtue. Where idiocy is a way of life, there can be no distancing from distancing, no grain against which to grow.

We live what Marx called the "ecstasy of political society" in the degree to which the individual person separates his personal intimate virtues and activities from his social or political identity.

That virtue be located within the separate, egoistic individual presupposes the experience of separation as most real and intimate, entails the bifurcation of "authentic man" from political man or citizen. "Authentic man" becomes "natural man" only in specific social conditions.

What we feel as most natural, Marx knew, was most social. The idea of the person as a self-sufficient monad, "withdrawn into himself, his private interest and private choice, separated from the community as a member of civil society" (*Young Marx*, p. 237) was for Marx the alienation of people from their species (social) life. The alienation of our collective, social life, projected outside of ourselves as "political society," is then seen as a limit on our freedom or "original independence," and this independence becomes the source of all value.

In this realm of identification, "man as bourgeois rather than man as citizen is considered to be the *proper* and *authentic* man." From this perspective we find in other people "not the realization but rather the limitation" of our freedom (*Young Marx*, pp. 237, 236). Thus the "ecstasy of political society," political society standing outside of us as the abstract state or system, is politics as it is understood in what I have called the condition of *extasis*.

The "politics" of such a condition is ecstatic, whether it is the organization of the "external" or the "internal" worlds of our experience. These two sides of ecstasy are what Marx understood as the "double life" of the fully developed political state: (1) the "innermost actuality," in everyday life of the proper or authentic self, an "illusory phenomenon," and (2) the "imaginary" membership in the sovereignty of the state (*Young Marx*, p. 226). The double life of people in this condition is the doubleness of illusion and imagination, illusory selfhood and imaginary citizenship.

Out of this condition Nietzsche developed his understanding of the "politics of virtue." Theodor Adorno wrote that Nietzsche did not live long enough to grow sick to his stomach at the jargon of authenticity. Yet it is also true that one of our most persuasive "authentic" understandings of what it means to be oneself is intelligible on Nietzschian grounds.

Nietzsche's politics of virtue is based on the attributes of what he called a Dionysian consciousness, which is the aesthetic understanding of experience possible at the edge of the marketplace.

148

Dionysian consciousness is characterized for Nietzsche by (1) its calmness: it involves the suspension of and "retardation of the feelings of time and space," that is, it is the aesthetic of contextlessness; and (2) its "simplification, abbreviation and contraction."

This ecstatic consciousness is a slowing down of the haste and hustle of the marketplace: "to react slowly; a great consciousness; no feeling of struggle" (*Power*, #799). The prose poem *Zarathustra* is Nietzsche's expression of the musical beauty of this consciousness which is the aesthetic of authenticity. Nietzsche said that perhaps the whole of *Zarathustra* may be reckoned as music, that "a rebirth of the act of hearing was among its preconditions": the precondition of the politics of virtue.

Slowing down of perception to a body consciousness which Nietzsche called "intelligent sensuality" is the Dionysian "refinement of the organs for the apprehension of much that is extremely small and fleeting." The feeling of strength and power of the healthy animal, "strength as a feeling of dominion in the muscles, ... as pleasure in the proof of strength, as bravado, adventure, fearlessness, indifference to life or death" (#800) was the basis of Nietzsche's aesthetic. Slowing down perception to see carefully and fully and with concentration involves the ". . . inability not to react" the "metamorphosis" of a distanced anaesthetic into an aesthetic being. The Dionysian urge "to unity, a reaching out beyond personality, the every day, society, reality, across the abyss of transitoriness" (#1050) is approximated through music, which Nietzsche saw as a remnant of the bodily representation and imitation of everything we feel. Music is possible as a "special art" only through the ordering and "immobilization" of the body's "muscle sense"; it is a specialization attained slowly "at the expense of those faculties which are most closely related to it" (#1050).

Any social order and all great art involve an immobilization of some part of the totality of our Dionysian consciousness. All such art is, from the perspective of Dionysus, a partiality, a fragment, culled from the "whole affective system" of human possibilities.

It is in this sense that Nietzsche saw people as fragments of the future, burdened by idols and values which limited strength and beauty. Music gives permission to touch the depth of Dionysian experience. It provides a particular perspective, like the music which can be heard in the solitude beyond the marketplace, where the buzzing and the distraction cease: the chirping of the cicadas, a pulse through the mountains, the rhythm of life, a lesson in the rebirth of the art of hearing.

Rebirth is a metaphor which is central to an understanding of Nietzsche's aesthetic, and its relation to the political psychology of permission. Since this psychology is the experience of the politics of idiotic virtue, the experience of rebirth connects the logic of this politics with the theory of permission, which, I think, is the central quality of Nietzsche's thought. Here I want to turn to the psychology of rebirth as Nietzsche understands it.

Becoming One's Own Heir: The Political Psychology of the Posthumous Man

Nietzsche said that he was a posthumous man, and he depicts Zarathustra as carrying his own ashes to the mountain. Death, the prerequisite to rebirth, was a counselor to Nietzsche, the shadow of his wanderings. Like Heidegger, he taught a doctrine of free death, the dying of an already posthumous man who has learned how to die because he has become his own child.

In order to experience the aesthetic of Dionysus, men who have grown up in the market culture of distraction must learn the consciousness of the child. This is the fundamental "metamorphosis" toward the affirmation of life and power which Nietzsche spoke of as the "game of creation," which only the child in man can play: "The child is innocence and forgetting, a new beginning, a game, a self-propelled wheel, a first movement, a sacred 'yes.' For the game of creation, my brothers, a sacred 'yes' is needed: the spirit now wills his own will, and he who had been lost to the world now conquers his own world" (*Zarathustra*, p. 139).

This child perspective is the new center which Nietzsche sought. This center was opposed to what he called "the spirit of gravity," the grave burdens of received "thou shalts," the shoulds which are the "Apollonian" limits of our moral experience. Apollo is the god of society, of moral, customary patterns which describe meaningful limits. Apollo in Greek mythology slays the dragon, nature. In Nietzsche's symbolism the lion, courage, is needed to slay the Apollonian (fear-inducing) dragon of "thou shalts" which weighs down the human spirit. This "burdened" spirit is what Nietzsche calls the "camel." The metamorphosis of the human spirit from camel to lion to child is the process of becoming a posthumous man.

This process is the unfolding of the narcissism of the owner, of the love through which "one can bear to be with onself and need not roam." The treasure of this self-love is *one's own:*

> For whatever is his own is well concealed from the
> owner; and of all treasures, it is our own that we dig up
> last: thus the spirit of gravity orders it. (*Zarathustra,*
> p. 305)

Nietzsche wrote: "But do you want to go the way of your afflic-tion, which is the way to yourself?" (p. 174). To have a "com-pleted world to give away" is the virtue which Nietzsche teaches. In order to have that virtue a man must have the courage for what he really knows, must face himself. We put it off through what Nietzsche called the "ways of self-narcotization":

> Deep down: not knowing whither. *Emptiness.* Attempt
> to get over it by intoxication: intoxication as music, . . .
> cruelty, . . . blind enthusiasm for single human beings or
> ages. . . . Attempt to work blindly as an instrument of
> science: opening one's eyes to the many small
> enjoyments; e.g., also in the quest for knowledge
> (modesty toward onself); resignation to generalizing
> about oneself, a pathos; mysticism, the voluptuous
> enjoyment of eternal emptiness; art "for its own sake" (*le
> fait*) and "pure knowledge" as narcotic states of disgust
> with oneself; some kind or other of continual work, or of
> some stupid little fanaticism. . . . (*Power,* #29)

Pick your virtue, pick your addiction.

The promise and the affliction, the wisdom and the idiocy, of the gift-giving virtue were expressed by Nietzsche in this vision of our world before its time:

> You that are lonely today, you who are withdrawing, you
> shall one day be the people. Out of you, who have
> chosen yourselves, there shall grow a chosen people.
> (*Zarathustra,* p. 189)

This seems to me to be the dominant thought of our age, where withdrawal becomes the social psychology of a people, the foun-dation for an ethos of autonomy. This ethos is at the basis of Nietzsche's political psychology of permission. To choose oneself, to become one's own, one must reparent oneself. For Nietzsche the fundamental question in politics is: Who are my parents, my ancestors? Nietzsche's answer is: I am.

To learn to see the world from the perspective of a reparented child is to learn to see with wonder and awe, detail and pleasure, to see the world as indistinguishable from the self, to know that all things are permitted. To want to become a child is to want it all: to want to be one's own mother and the pain of one's own birth:

> Indeed, there must be much bitter dying in your life,
> you creators. Thus you are advocates and justifiers of all
> impermanence. To be the child who is newly born, the
> creator must also want to be the mother who gives birth
> and the pangs of the birth-giver. (*Zarathustra*, p. 199)

To become one's own parent and to become one's own child are two ways of describing the same project. Dylan's line "But I was so much older then, I'm younger than that now" is a contemporary expression of this project. Nietzsche saw and praised these characteristics in Ralph Waldo Emerson:

> ... he simply does not know how old he is already and
> how young he is still going to be; he could say of
> himself, quoting Lope de Vega: "yo me sucedo a mi
> mismo" (I am my own heir). (*Twilight*, p. 522)

To become one's own heir is to take the essence of morals—the inheritance of patterns of meaning and value—and locate it within the self. The location of the moral world within the self is the basic aspect of the political psychology of permission. But the only "world" which is in fact "located" in this way is a dream world. Dreaming was, for Nietzsche, the compulsion in the human animal "to have visions, a dream state which releases the powers of vision, association, poetry" (*Power*, #798). This Apollonian compulsion is both the form of the world of everyday distraction, of the spirit of gravity, and as well the root of any "vision beyond" that world, the *source* of vision, association, and poetry. The experience of becoming one's own mother is a dream experience which is the interior state of receiving "permission," of understanding that all things are permitted. It is a reaching into the unconscious.

In Jungian dream interpretation, Mother is symbolic of the collective unconscious, of the nocturnal side of existence—the source of the "Water of Life," or what Nietzsche called the will to power.

The political psychology of permission is a dream state beyond all danger and fear. "Permission dreams" are dreams which open access to the understanding that all things are permitted. Here is an example from my own experience of a permission dream:

> I am standing next to three other men by an open window looking out to sea. The men are all very strong, powerful (not physically). I have only the feeling of presence about me there, looking out. I am not self-conscious. The waves which are coming in toward the window are greenish-white, looking partly like snow, sand, and water. They are overwhelmingly beautiful and I stand and watch them as they break, on the diagonal, toward the window, with awe. Next to me, on my right and slightly behind me is the presence of Mother. Not *my* mother, but the feeling of total permission. One enormous wave crashes in and Mother says, "It's time to go." Deep death feeling. I dive, along with the three other men (no feeling of fear or competition or performance) out of the window. But not into the sea, rather I feel a wind blowing as soon as I jump and it pushes me out, I fly against it, turn left toward the other men, and we fly together over the waves.

The dream state of permission contrasts sharply with the state of self-disgust in which narcissistic images are disowned. Nietzsche relates one of Zarathustra's dreams:

> Why was I so startled in my dream that I awoke? Did not a child step up to me, carrying a mirror? "Oh, Zarathustra," the child said to me, "look at yourself in the mirror." But when I looked into the mirror I cried out, and my heart was shaken: for it was not myself I saw, but a devil's grimace and scornful laughter. (*Zarathustra*, p. 195)

Fear of what the child will show you about yourself is rooted in the desire to maintain control, to dominate or repress the child. I once dreamed that I was alone in my parents' house, hearing sounds of young adolescents in the basement. I got my father's rifle, went to the basement door, and unlocked it. The door opened and a beautiful young child stood there with arms out-reached toward me, crouching. I pointed the rifle at the child and said "Hold it!" As I did so the child became me, and I saw myself pointing the rifle at myself. I knew the rifle was not loaded, and I awoke.

Not to be ashamed or disgusted before oneself was what Nietzsche understood as freedom. In the political theory of permission, freedom is a relationship with oneself: "What is the seal of attained freedom?," Nietzsche asked: "No longer being ashamed in front of oneself" (*Morals*, p. 293; [Aphorism #275 from *The Gay Science*]). To speak of shame before oneself means that a relationship between people has been interiorized as a relationship of the self to itself. Thus Nietzsche knew that a good deal of that which is our own are the "shoulds" of morality (". . . much that is our *own* is also a grave burden!"). That there is an internal political dialogue within the self which is predominantly between parent and child is the central proposition of the political psychology of permission. The "subject" of that dialogue is guilt, that is, internalized shame. This subject is the stuff which is held back behind its activities, the powerlessness of the oppressed, the "self-deception" of the guilty conscience or "soul" (*Morals*, p. 46).

This is what Nietzsche calls the "internalization" of man, the creation of an inner world of hostility, cruelty, joy in persecuting, attacking, changing, and destroying oneself. This creation is political for Nietzsche in the sense in which "political organization," through institutions of punishment, turns the human instinct for freedom against itself (*Morals*, p. 84).

But, as Nietzsche put it, "We immoralists prefer not to believe in guilt" (*Power*, #235). Guilt was possible, Nietzsche thought, as "an experience derived from nature or society universalized and projected into the sphere of the 'in-itself' " (#579). The guilty conscience, however, was for Nietzsche "pregnant with a future," the future of autonomy. The social experience of being a beast of burden (the camel is his metaphor, weighted down by the spirit of gravity, the "thou shalts" of morality), out of which guilt is accumulated and stored within and against the self, can be overcome through resistance, through courage and will. To create a space of freedom for oneself "for new creation" is to say no to the spirit of the "thou shalt," to let go of the "true" world, to receive permission. To unlearn the fearful defensiveness and self-denial of the guilty conscience is a political act. The narcissistic rediscovery of the self which is beyond good and evil, which is in touch with its power as capacity, is incompatible with a particular sort of political order, the experience of which I have called "living in danger."

Danger, we have seen, is the privilege of the moral animal. Nietzsche understood that it was dangerous to be an heir. The genealogy of danger is for Nietzsche rooted in *"fear of the ancestor and his power"* (*Morals*, p. 89). The power of the ancestor is domination, the power of the lord or master. Fear of this power is the mother of morals. It is in this sense that the political psychology of permission is immoral: it stands in opposition to danger.

The situation of danger is what I would call a "performance" context, one wherein the desire to please, entertain, distract, placate a *dan* out of fear and in order to achieve praise constitutes the experience of domination. For Nietzsche, the gift-giving virtue was beyond danger:

> When you are above praise and blame, and your will
> wants to command all things, like a lover's will: there is
> the origin of your virtue. (*Zarathustra*, p. 188)

But, for Nietzsche, the destiny of such a virtue was catastrophe:

> I love him who makes his virtue his addiction and his
> catastrophe: for his virtue's sake he wants to live on and
> to live no longer. (*Zarathustra*, p. 189)

To become your own ancestor, your own heir, to love yourself, to cease to be your own contemporary, is to become your own danger; it is a catastrophe, an idiocy, the wretchedness of those who can *only* give:

> My happiness in giving died in giving: my virtue tired of
> itself in its overflow. (*Zarathustra*, p. 218)

The danger of those who always give is that they lose their sense of shame, and "the heart and hand of those who always mete out become callous from always meting out" (*Zarathustra*, p. 218). Thus it is that the virtue becomes an addiction, an obsession, and finally a catastrophe. Pressed to the limit, idiocy seeks companions; the private and separate person internalizes as much as can be taken within the self, becomes a child, and dies of his own virtue.

Thus it is that the Nietzsche who understood the obsession with owness and lived it fully, discovered that the self which can be one's own ceased by that very logic to perpetrate its idiocy:

> What I always required most, however, for my cure and
> self-recovery, was the belief that I was *not* isolated in
> such circumstances, that I did not *see* in an isolated
> manner—a magic suspicion of relationship and similarity
> to others in outlook and desire, a repose in the
> confidence of friendship. . . . (*Human All-Too-Human*,
> p. 2)

Nietzsche understood that there is no " 'being' behind doing, ef-
fecting, becoming; 'the doer' is merely a fiction added to the
deed—the deed is everything" (*Morals*, p. 45). No secret, subjective, hidden self in there, in private behind our masks. The internalization of man, of freedom, community, one's ancestors, the
owning up to it all as what we have chosen to be, is a history
which could be told (as Rousseau did in the *Discourse on the Origins of Inequality*) as the development of the *idea* of private property applied to human identity. This recognition does not lead
Nietzsche to conclude that we must live within ourselves. To attempt this is an illusion, a perspective which would make the self
into a fetish and obsession. Where the state and the marketplace
end, idiots, jesters, corpses, and convalescents cry out: "Must not
lanterns be lit in the morning?" (*Gay Science*, #125, p. 95). To try
to find *my* way, I must have companions. Such a motley crew, you
say, but put it in perspective:

> . . . to *want* to see differently, is no small discipline and
> preparation of the intellect for its future "objectivity."
> . . . There is only a perspective seeing, only a
> perspective "knowing"; and the more affects we allow to
> speak about one thing, the *more* eyes, different eyes, we
> can use to observe one thing, the more complete will our
> "concept" of this thing, our "objectivity" be (*Morals*,
> p. 119)

Afterword

I have written this book in the conviction that idiocy is the preparation of our future "objectivity," in Nietzsche's sense, and in Marx's sense as well:

> A being which has no object outside itself is not
> objective. . . . A non-objective being is an unactual,
> non-sensuous, merely conceived being. It is merely
> imagined, an abstraction. (*Young Marx*, p. 326)

When Marx noted that private property had made us so stupid that we could conceive of no meaning apart from possession or having, he added:

> Human nature had to be reduced to this absolute
> poverty so that it could give birth to its inner wealth.
> (*Young Marx*, p. 308)

On the basis of the absolute poverty of the self as private property we can judge something of what we are being prepared for. I have written this book in order to reveal the poverty that is the ground of our wealth. I have written to those who *want* to see differently, in the hope of companionship from what Nietzsche called "preparatory men":

> . . . men characterized by cheerfulness, patience,
> unpretentiousness and contempt for all vanities, as well
> as by magnanimity in victory and forbearance regarding
> the small vanities of the vanquished . . . men who have
> their own festivals, their own weekdays, their own
> periods of mourning . . . men who are in greater danger,
> more fruitful and happier! . . . Soon the age will be past
> when you could be satisfied to live like shy deer, hidden
> in the woods! At long last the pursuit of knowledge will
> reach out for its due: it will want to *rule* and *own*, and
> you with it. (*Gay Science*, #293, p. 98)

This is the pathos and the poetry of the self as private property.

Reference Titles Used in Source Notes

For full information, see the Bibliography.

Abnormal Psychology. Davidson and Neale.
Accidental. Harrington, *The A. Century*.
Acquistion. Merleau-Ponty, *Consciousness and the A. of Language*.
Anxiety. Auden, *The Age of A.*
Archeology. Foucault, *The A. of Knowledge*.
Authenticity. Berman, *The Politics of A.*
Bacon Selected. Bacon, *S. Writings*.
Behemoth. Hobbes.
Being and Having. Marcel.
Being and Nothingness. Sartre.
Being and Time. Heidegger.
Best Friend. Newman and Berkowitz, *How to Be Your Own B. F.*
Betrayal. Lowen, *The B. of the Body*.
Beyond Freedom. Skinner, *B. F. and Dignity*.
Boundaries. Lifton.
Brother Animal. Roazen.
Child's Conception. Piaget, *The C. C. of the World*.
Christianity. Hegel, *On C., Early Theological Writings*.
City of God. Augustine.
Civilization. Freud, *C. and Its Discontents*.
Classic American. Lawrence, *Studies of C. A. Literature*.
Collected Papers. Fenichel.
Common Sense. Paine, *C. S. and Other Political Writings*.
Corporation. Berle and Means, *The Modern C. and Private Property*.
Cybernetic. Parsegian, *This C. World*.
Democracy. Tocqueville, *D. in America*.
Dialogues. Plato, *The D. of P.*
Discourses. Machiavelli, in *The Prince and The D.*
Discourses. Rousseau, *The First and Second D.*
Discovery. Snell, *The D. of the Mind*.
Dread. Kierkegaard, *The Concept of D.*
Duration. Bergson, *D. and Simultaneity*.
Ego. Stirner, *The E. and His Own*.
Either/Or. Kierkegaard.
Emerson Selections. Emerson, *S. from Ralph Waldo E.*
Emile. Rousseau.
Errand. Miller, *E. into the Wilderness*.
Ethics. Aristotle, *The E. of A.*
Existentialism. Wahl, *A Short History of E.*

REFERENCE TITLES

Fear. Kierkegaard, *F. and Trembling and The Sickness Unto Death.*
Federalist. Rossiter, ed., *The F. Papers.*
Gay Science. Nietzsche.
Gestalt. Perls, *G. Therapy Verbatim.*
Gift. Mauss.
Good and Evil. Nietzsche, *Beyond G. and E.*
History of Philosophy. Hegel, *Lectures of the H. of P.*
Human. Arendt, *The H. Condition.*
Human All-Too-Human. Nietzsche.
Imperial. Anderson, *The I. Self.*
Institutes. Calvin, *I. of the Christian Religion.*
Jargon. Adorno, *The J. of Authenticity.*
Journals. Kierkegaard, *The J. of K.*
Leaves of Grass. Whitman.
Leviathan. Hobbes.
Liberal Tradition. Hartz, *The L. T. in America.*
Life. Brown, *L. against Death.*
Love's Body. Brown.
Luther Selections. Martin L.: S. from His Writings.
Madness. Foucault, *M. and Civilization.*
Marx Selected. Marx, *Karl M.: S. Writings in Sociology and Social Philosophy.*
Mary Barnes. Barnes and Berke.
Mind. Hegel, *The Phenomenology of M.*
Morals. Nietzsche, *On the Genealogy of M.*
Myth and Guilt. Reik.
Pedagogy. Friere, *The P. of the Oppressed.*
Perception. Merleau-Ponty, *The Phenomenology of P.*
Philosophical Writings. Descartes.
Philosophy of History. Hegel.
Political Thought. Barker, *The P. T. of Plato and Aristotle.*
Political Writings. Adams, *The P. W. of John A.*
Politics. Aristotle, *The P. of A.*
Politics of the Family. Laing, *The P. of the F. and Other Essays.*
Possessed. Dostoyevsky.
Possessive Individualism. MacPherson, *The Political Theory of P. I.*
Post Industrial. Bell, *The Coming of the P. I. Society.*
Postscript. Kierkegaard, *Concluding Unscientific P.*
Power. Nietzsche, *The Will to Power.*
Power Elite. Mills, *The Power Elite.*
Present Age. Kierkegaard.
Primitive. Lévy-Bruhl, *The P. Mentality.*
Prince. Machiavelli, *The P. and The Discourses.*
Psychology of Being. Maslow, *Toward a P. of B.*
Puritans. Miller, *The American P.*
Reality. Castaneda, *A Separate R.*
Reason and Revolution. Marcuse.
Republic. Plato, *The R. of P.*
Right. Hegel's Philosophy of Right.
Saints. Walzer, *The Revolution of the S.*
Sane. Fromm, *The S. Society.*

REFERENCE TITLES

Sanity. Laing and Esterson, *S., Madness, and the Family.*
Scripts. Steiner, *S. People Live.*
Sense. Merleau-Ponty, *S. and Non-Sense.*
Service. Fuchs, *The S. Economy.*
Sickness. Kierkegaard, in *Fear and Trembling and The S. Unto Death.*
Signs. Merleau-Ponty.
Six Plays. Ibsen, *S. P. by Henrik I.*
Social Basis. Burrow, *The S. B. of Consciousness.*
Social Behavior. Homans.
Social Contract. Rousseau.
Solitude. Powys, *A Philosophy of S.*
Therapy. Freud, *T. and Technique.*
Time. Bergson, *T. and Free Will.*
Totem. Freud, *T. and Taboo.*
Tragedy. Nietzsche, *The Birth of T.*
Transformation. Polanyi, *The Great T.*
Twilight. Nietzsche, *T. of the Idols.*
Violence. Sorel, *Reflections on V.*
Walden. Thoreau, *W. and Other Writings.*
Young Marx. Marx, *Writings of the Y. M. on Philosophy and Society.*
Zarathustra. Nietzsche, *Thus Spake Z.*

Bibliography

Adams, John. *The Political Writings of John Adams,* ed. G. Peek. Indianapolis: Bobbs-Merrill, 1954. Reference: *Political Writings.*

Adorno, T. *The Jargon of Authenticity.* Evanston, Ill.: Northwestern University Press, 1973. Reference: *Jargon.*

Anderson, Q. *The Imperial Self.* New York: Knopf, 1971. Reference: *Imperial.*

Arendt, H. *The Human Condition.* New York: Doubleday Anchor Books, 1969. Reference: *Human.*

Aristotle. *The Ethics of Aristotle,* tr. J. A. K. Thomson. London: Allen and Unwin, 1953. Reference: *Ethics.*

Aristotle. *The Politics of Aristotle,* ed. and tr. E. Barker. New York: Oxford University Press, 1972. Reference: *Politics.*

Auden, W. H. *The Age of Anxiety.* New York: Random House, 1947. Reference: *Anxiety.*

Augustine. *The City of God,* tr. T. Merton. New York: Modern Library, 1950. Reference: *City of God.*

Ausker, P. "One-Man Language." *New York Review of Books,* 22:1 (January 1975), 30-31.

Bacon, Francis. *Selected Writings.* New York: Modern Library, 1957. Reference: *Bacon Selected.*

Barker, E. *The Political Thought of Plato and Aristotle.* New York: Dover, 1959. Reference: *Political Thought.*

Barnes, M., and J. Berke. *Mary Barnes: Two Accounts of a Journey through Madness.* New York: Harcourt Brace Jovanovich, 1972. Reference: *Mary Barnes.*

Bell, Daniel. *The Coming of the Post-Industrial Society: A Venture in Social Forecasting.* New York: Basic Books, 1973. Reference: *Post-Industrial.*

Bellow, S. "On Boredom." *New York Review of Books,* 22:13 (7 August 1975), 22.

Bergson, H. *Duration and Simultaneity.* New York: Library of Liberal Arts, 1965. Reference: *Duration.*

Bergson, H. *Time and Free Will.* New York: Harper Torchbooks, 1960. Reference: *Time.*

Berle, A. A., and G. C. Means. *The Modern Corporation and Private Property.* New York: Harcourt Brace Jovanovich, 1967. Reference: *Corporation.*

Berman, M. *The Politics of Authenticity.* New York: Atheneum, 1972. Reference: *Authenticity.*

Binswanger, L. "Heidegger's Analytic and Its Meaning for Psychiatry." In *Being-In-the-World,* ed. J. Needleman. New York: Basic Books, 1963.

Brown, N. O. *Life against Death: The Psychoanalytic Meaning of History.* Middletown, Conn.: Wesleyan University Press, 1959. Reference: *Life.*

Brown, N. O. *Love's Body.* New York: Vintage Books, 1966. Reference: *Love's Body.*

Burrow, T. *The Social Basis of Consciousness.* New York: Harcourt Brace Jovanovich, 1972. Reference: *Social Basis.*

Calvin, John. *Institutes of the Christian Religion,* tr. F. W. Battles. Philadelphia: Westminster Press, 1960. Reference: *Institutes.*

BIBLIOGRAPHY

Castaneda, C. *A Separate Reality*. New York: Simon and Schuster, 1971. Reference: *Reality*.

Cottle, T. J. "The Sexual Revolution and the Young—Four Studies." *New York Times Magazine*, 26 November 1972.

Davidson, G. C., and J. M. Neale. *Abnormal Psychology: An Experimental, Clinical Approach*. New York: Wiley, 1974. Reference: *Abnormal*.

Descartes, René. *Philosophical Writings*, tr. N. K. Smith. New York: Modern Library, 1958. Reference: *Philosophical Writings*.

Dostoyevsky, F. *The Possessed*. New York: Modern Library, 1936. Reference: *Possessed*.

Draguns, J., and L. Phillips. *Culture and Psychopathology: The Quest for a Relationship*. Morristown, N.J.: General Learning Press, 1972.

Dylan, Bob. "Dirge." From *Planet Waves*. New York: Ram's Horn Music, ASCAP, Asylum Record, Warner Communications, Inc., 1974.

Emerson, R. W. *Selections from Ralph Waldo Emerson*, ed. S. Whicher. New York: Houghton Mifflin, 1960. Reference: *Emerson Selections*.

Fenichel, O. "On the Psychology of Boredom." In *Collected Papers*. New York: Norton, 1953-1954.

Foucault, M. *The Archeology of Knowledge*, tr. A. M. Sheridan Smith. New York: Pantheon Books, 1972. Reference: *Archeology*.

Foucault, M. *Madness and Civilization*, tr. R. Howard. New York: Pantheon Books, 1965. Reference: *Madness*.

Freud, Sigmund. *Civilization and Its Discontents*. New York: Norton, 1959. Reference: *Civilization*.

Freud, Sigmund. *Therapy and Technique*, ed. P. Reiff. New York: Collier Books, 1967. Reference: *Therapy*.

Freud, Sigmund. *Totem and Taboo*, Standard Ed. V. XIII. New York: Hogarth Press, 1950. Reference: *Totem*.

Friere, P. *The Pedagogy of the Oppressed*. New York: Herder, 1972. Reference: *Pedagogy*.

Fromm, E. *The Sane Society*. New York: Fawcett, 1955. Reference: *Sane*.

Fuchs, V. R. *The Service Economy*. New York: National Bureau for Economic Research/Columbia University Press, 1968. Reference: *Service*.

Galt, W. "Our Mother Tongue: Etymological Implications of the Social Neurosis." *Psychoanalytic Review*, 30:3 (July 1943).

Glass, J. "Schizophrenia and Perception: A Critique of the Liberal Theory of Externality." *Inquiry*, 15 (1972), 114-145.

Harrington, M. *The Accidental Century*. New York: Macmillan, 1965. Reference: *Accidental*.

Hartz, L. *The Liberal Tradition in America: An Interpretation of American Political Thought since the Revolution*. New York: Harcourt Brace Jovanovich, 1962. Reference: *Liberal Tradition*.

Hegel, G. W. F. *On Christianity, Early Theological Writings*, tr. T. M. Knox. New York: Harper Torchbooks, 1967. Reference: *Christianity*.

Hegel, G. W. F. *Hegel's Lectures on the History of Philosophy*, tr. E. S. Haldane. London: Routledge, 1955. Reference: *History of Philosophy*.

Hegel, G. W. F. *The Phenomenology of Mind*, tr. J. B. Baillie. New York: Harper Torchbooks, 1967. Reference: *Mind*.

Hegel, G. W. F. *The Philosophy of History*, tr. J. Sibree. New York: Collier, 1900. Reference: *Philosophy of History*.

BIBLIOGRAPHY

Hegel's Philosophy of Right, tr. with notes by T. M. Knox. Oxford: Clarendon, 1949. Reference: *Right*.

Heidegger, M. *Being and Time*, tr. J. Macquarie and E. Robinson. New York: Harper, 1962. Reference: *Being and Time*.

Hobbes, T. *Behemoth*. New York: Burt Franklin, 1963. Reference: *Behemoth*.

Hobbes, T. *Leviathan*. New York: Collier Books, 1966. Reference: *Leviathan*.

Homans, G. C. *Social Behavior: Its Elementary Forms*. New York: Harcourt Brace Jovanovich, 1974. Reference: *Social Behavior*.

Ibsen, H. *Six Plays by Henrik Ibsen*. New York: Modern Library, 1958. Reference: *Six Plays*.

Kierkegaard, S. *The Concept of Dread*, tr. W. Lowrie. 2nd ed. Princeton, N.J.: Princeton University Press, 1967. Reference: *Dread*.

Kierkegaard, S. *Concluding Unscientific Postscript*, tr. W. Lowrie. Princeton, N.J.: Princeton University Press, 1960. Reference: *Postscript*.

Kierkegaard, S. *Either/Or*, tr. D. F. and L. M. Swenson. Garden City, N.Y.: Doubleday Anchor Books, 1959. Reference: *Either/Or*.

Kierkegaard, S. *Fear and Trembling and The Sickness Unto Death*, tr. W. Lowrie. Princeton, N.J.: Princeton University Press, 1969. References: *Fear, Sickness*.

Kierkegaard, S. *The Journals of Kierkegaard*, tr. A. Dru. New York: Harper Torchbooks, 1959. Reference: *Journals*.

Kierkegaard, S. *The Present Age*. New York: Harper Torchbooks, 1959. Reference: *Present Age*.

Laing, R. D. *The Politics of the Family and Other Essays*. New York: Pantheon, 1971. Reference: *Politics of the Family*.

Laing, R. D., and A. Esterson. *Sanity, Madness, and the Family*. New York: Penguin, 1970. Reference: *Sanity*.

Lawrence, D. H. *Studies in Classic American Literature*. New York: Viking, 1964. Reference: *Classic American*.

Lévy-Bruhl, L. *The Primitive Mentality*. London: Allen and Unwin, 1923. Reference: *Primitive*.

Lifton, R. J. *Boundaries*. New York: Vintage Books, 1970. Reference: *Boundaries*.

Lowen, A. *The Betrayal of the Body*. New York: Collier Books, 1967. Reference: *Betrayal*.

Luther, Martin. *Martin Luther: Selections from His Writings*, ed. J. Dillenberger. New York: Doubleday Anchor Books, 1961. Reference: *Luther Selections*.

Machiavelli, N. *The Prince and The Discourses*. New York: Modern Library, 1950. References: *Prince, Discourses*.

MacPherson, C. B. *The Political Theory of Possessive Individualism: From Hobbes to Locke*. London: Oxford University Press, 1962. Reference: *Possessive Individualism*.

Marcel, G. *Being and Having*. New York: Harper Torchbooks, 1960. Reference: *Being and Having*.

Marcuse, H. *Reason and Revolution: Hegel and the Rise of Social Theory*. Boston: Beacon, 1968. Reference: *Reason and Revolution*.

Marx, Karl. *Karl Marx: Selected Writings in Sociology and Social Philosophy*, tr. and ed. T. B. Bottomore and M. Rubel. New York: McGraw-Hill, 1964. Reference: *Marx Selected*.

Marx, Karl. *Writings of the Young Marx on Philosophy and Society*, tr. L. D. Easton and K. H. Guddat. New York: Doubleday Anchor Books, 1967. Reference: *Young Marx*.

BIBLIOGRAPHY

Maslow, A. *Toward a Psychology of Being*. Princeton, N. J.: Van Nostrand, 1962. Reference: *Psychology of Being*.

Mauss, M. *The Gift: Forms and Functions of Exchange in Archaic Societies*. New York: Norton, 1966. Reference: *Gift*.

Merleau-Ponty, M. *Consciousness and the Acquisition of Language*, tr. H. J. Silverman. Evanston, Ill.: Northwestern University Press, 1973. Reference: *Acquisition*.

Merleau-Ponty, M. *The Phenomenology of Perception*, tr. C. Smith. New York: Humanities Press, 1962. Reference: *Perception*.

Merleau-Ponty, M. *Sense and Non-Sense*, tr. H. and P. Dreyfus. Evanston, Ill.: Northwestern University Press, 1964. Reference: *Sense*.

Merleau-Ponty, M. *Signs*, tr. R. McCleary. Evanston, Ill.: Northwestern University Press, 1964. Reference: *Signs*.

Miller, P., ed. *The American Puritans: Their Prose and Poetry*. Garden City, N.Y.: Doubleday, 1956. Reference: *Puritans*.

Miller, P. *Errand into the Wilderness*. New York: Harper Torchbook, 1959. Reference: *Errand*.

Mills, C. Wright. *The Power Elite*. New York: Oxford University Press, 1959. Reference: *Power Elite*.

Newman, M., and B. Berkowitz. *How to Be Your Own Best Friend*. New York: Ballantine Books, 1974. Reference: *Best Friend*.

Nietzsche, F. *Beyond Good and Evil: Prelude to a Philosophy of the Future*, tr. W. Kaufmann. New York: Vintage Books, 1966. Reference: *Good and Evil*.

Nietzsche, F. *The Birth of Tragedy and The Case of Wagner*, tr. W. Kaufmann. New York: Vintage Books, 1967. Reference: *Tragedy*.

Nietzsche, F. *The Gay Science*. In *The Portable Nietzsche*, ed. and tr. W. Kaufmann. New York: Viking, 1963. Reference: *Gay Science*.

Nietzsche, F. *On the Genealogy of Morals*, tr. W. Kaufmann and R. J. Hollingdale. New York: Vintage Books, 1969. Reference: *Morals*.

Nietzsche, F. *Human All-Too-Human*, tr. H. Zimmern. Volume 6 of *The Complete Works of Friedrich Nietzsche*, ed. O. Levy, London: T. N. Foulis, 1910.

Nietzsche, F. *Thus Spake Zarathustra*. In *The Portable Nietzsche*, tr. and ed. W. Kaufmann. New York: Viking, 1970. Reference: *Zarathustra*.

Nietzsche, F. *Twilight of the Idols*. In *The Portable Nietzsche*, ed. and tr. W. Kaufmann. New York: Viking, 1963. Reference: *Twilight*.

Nietzsche, F. *The Will to Power*, tr. W. Kaufmann. New York: Vintage Books, 1968. Reference: *Power*.

Paine, T. *Common Sense and Other Political Writings*, ed. N. F. Adkins. New York: Liberal Arts Press, 1953. Reference: *Common Sense*.

Parsegian, V. L. *This Cybernetic World*. New York: Doubleday Anchor Books, 1973. Reference: *Cybernetic*.

Perls, F. *Gestalt Therapy Verbatim*. New York: Bantam Books, 1969. Reference: *Gestalt*.

Piaget, J. *The Child's Conception of the World*. Totowa, N.J.: Littlefield, Adams, 1967. Reference: *Child's Conception*.

Plato. *The Dialogues of Plato*, tr. B. Jowett. New York: Scribner, 1960. Reference: *Dialogues*.

Plato. *The Republic of Plato*, tr. A. Bloom. New York: Basic Books, 1968. Reference: *Republic*.

BIBLIOGRAPHY

Polanyi, K. *The Great Transformation*. Boston: Beacon Press, 1974. Reference: *Transformation*.

Powys, J. *A Philosophy of Solitude*. New York: Simon and Schuster, 1933. Reference: *Solitude*.

Reik, T. *Myth and Guilt*. New York: Grosset, 1962. Reference: *Myth and Guilt*.

Roazen, P. *Brother Animal*. New York: Knopf, 1969. Reference: *Brother Animal*.

Rosen, S. "Sophrosune and Selbstbewusstsein." *Review of Metaphysics*, 26 (June 1973), 617-642.

Rosenbaum, R. "Secrets of the Little Blue Box." *Esquire*, 76 (October 1971), 116-125+.

Rossiter, C., ed. *The Federalist Papers*. New York: Mentor Books, 1961. Reference: *Federalist*.

Rotenstreich, N. "On the Ecstatic Sources of the Concept of 'Alienation.'" *Review of Metaphysics*, 16 (March 1963), 550-555.

Rousseau, J. J. *Emile*, tr. B. Foxley. New York: Everyman's Library, 1914. Reference: *Emile*.

Rousseau, J. J. *The First and Second Discourses*, tr. and ed. R. D. Masters. New York: St. Martin's, 1964. Reference: *Discourses*.

Rousseau, J. J. *The Social Contract*, tr. G. D. H. Cole. New York: Dutton, 1961. Reference: *Social Contract*.

Rubinoff, L. "The Dialectic of Work and Labour." *Humanitas*, 7:2 (Fall 1971).

Sartre, J. P. *Being and Nothingness*, tr. H. Barnes. New York: Philosophical Library, 1956. Reference: *Being and Nothingness*.

Sartre, J. P. "Une idée fondamentale de la phénoménologie de Husserl: L'Intentionnalité. In *Situations I*, Paris: Gallimard, 1947, pp. 31-35.

Skinner, B. F. "Beyond Freedom and Dignity." Prepublication in *Psychology Today* (August 1971).

Skinner, B. F. *Beyond Freedom and Dignity*. New York: Knopf, 1972. Reference: *Beyond Freedom*.

Snell, B. *The Discovery of the Mind*. New York: Harper Torchbooks, 1960. Reference: *Discovery*.

Sorel, G. *Reflections on Violence*. New York: Collier Books, 1961. Reference: *Violence*.

Steiner, C. *Scripts People Live*. New York: Grove, 1974. Reference: *Scripts*.

Stirner, M. *The Ego and His Own*, tr. S. Byington. London: A. C. Fifield, 1913. Reference: *Ego*.

Storch, A. "The Primitive Archaic Forms of Inner Experiences and Thoughts in Schizophrenia." *Neurology and Mental Disorder Monograph Series*, 22, 1.

Strong, T. "Hold Onto Your Brains." In *Power and Community*, ed. P. Green and S. Levinson. New York: Pantheon, 1970.

Thoreau, H. D. *Walden and Other Writings of Henry David Thoreau*, ed. B. Atkinson. New York: Modern Library, 1937. Reference: *Walden*.

Tocqueville, A. de. *Democracy in America*, ed. P. Bradley. New York: Vintage Books, 1945. Reference: *Democracy*.

Wahl, J. *A Short History of Existentialism*. New York: Philosophical Library, 1949. Reference: *Existentialism*.

Waltzer, M. *The Revolution of the Saints*. Cambridge, Mass.: Harvard University Press, 1965. Reference: *Saints*.

Warren, T. H. "A Concept of Citizenship for America: An Essay on the Logic of Self-Reference." Conference paper, prospectus.

BIBLIOGRAPHY

White, W. "The Language of Schizophrenia." *Archives of Neurology and Psychiatry*, 16:4 (October 1926).

Whitman, W. *Leaves of Grass*, ed. S. Bradley. New York: Holt, 1949. Reference: *Leaves of Grass*.

Index